The Reader

AN INTRODUCTION TO
ORAL INTERPRETATION

for Todd and Alan

The Reader

AN INTRODUCTION TO

ORAL INTERPRETATION

DONALD N. WALTERS

CARL A. RUDISILL LIBRARY
LENOIR RHYNE COLLEGE

The Odyssey Press, Inc.   New York

ACKNOWLEDGMENTS

For excerpts from copyrighted materials appearing in this book, the author is indebted to the following authors, publishers, and agents:

Sherwood Anderson's "I'm a Fool", from HORSES AND MEN. Copyright 1924 by Eleanor Anderson. Copyright renewed. Reprinted by permission of Harold Ober Associates, Inc.

Charles Laughton's "Storytelling". Copyright © 1950 by The Atlantic Monthly Company, Boston, Mass. Reprinted by permission of Elsa Lanchester Laughton.

Leonard Q. Ross' THE EDUCATION OF HYMAN KAPLAN. Copyright 1937 by Harcourt, Brace & World, Inc., and reprinted with their permission.

Aldous Huxley's "Music at Night". Copyright 1931, © 1959 by Aldous Huxley. Reprinted by permission of Harper & Row, Publishers, Inc.

Audie Murphy's TO HELL AND BACK. Copyright 1949 by Holt, Rinehart and Winston, Inc., and reprinted with their permission.

James Baldwin's "Stranger in the Village", from NOTES OF A NATIVE SON. Copyright © 1953, 1955 by James Baldwin. Reprinted by permission of the Beacon Press.

Dylan Thomas' "Poetic Manifesto". © 1961 by the Estate of Dylan Thomas. Published in the Winter, 1961, issue of *The Texas Quarterly*, and reprinted by permission of the Trustees of the Estate of Dylan Thomas.

Arthur Miller's AFTER THE FALL. Copyright © 1964 by Arthur Miller. Reprinted by permission of The Viking Press, Inc.

Preface

This brief book is designed to introduce you to the principles of oral interpretation, or reading aloud. The text was written with three basic considerations in mind: (1) that the first chapter should relate the reading to the **speech;** (2) that the remainder of the work should describe the principles of reading aloud in terms of the reader's **performance;** and (3) that an awareness of the reader's relationship with his **audience** is the best guide a person can have, aside from the guidance of an instructor, in developing his abilities in reading aloud.

To illustrate the importance of this third consideration—that is, an awareness of the audience—I will cite an experience which reflects a professional reader's attitude toward his audience.

Several years ago, I was asked to escort a well-known actor to a theatre in my community which had secured the gentleman's talents for an evening of dramatic and lyric poetry reading. En route to the theatre, this actor's enthusiasm for literature so everwhelmed me that I was quite content to let him do all the talking —fortunately, for I learned something of value.

I particularly remember the actor's comments on Shelley's "Ode to the West Wind." Having pointed out some of the poem's merits, he concluded by saying that it was his favorite work by Shelley. I asked if he would be reading the poem in his program, and he replied, "Oh, no! It's too cold, too impersonal. I don't know that my audience would stand for it."

Apparently, this actor desired a deep emotional bond with his audience, for his readings made a strong emotional appeal that evening. Although he had great regard for "Ode to the West Wind," the poem was not suited to *his* objective as a reader, and he appeared determined to use only those writings that were in keeping with his idea of what a reading experience should be.

Your course through the pages that follow will introduce you to an idea of what a reading experience should be. You will likely discover, after the first few readings, how great a role the audience plays in the reading. It is likely you will also discover that reading aloud is a rewarding and enriching social experience.

D. N. W.

Contents

Chapter One

THE TALK AND THE READING

Following a speech class one day, a student told me about a talk he had heard while in the military service. The young man had neglected to make up his bed properly, and had been invited to be an audience of one for the oratory of the Sergeant Major.

The student said that he was "read the Riot Act" by the Sergeant. Although the experience was not an agreeable one, the young man admitted that the Sergeant possessed some "mighty powerful arguments" and did a good job of making his points lucid and memorable. Needless to say, the young man's bed was made up properly thereafter.

Of course, the rendering of the "Riot Act" was not a *reading,* as anyone who has been "read" this piece of legislation would know. More than likely, the young man had experienced a vigorous extemporaneous speech, or talk.

TALK AND READING SIMILARITIES

If you were asked to list the similarities between a talk and a reading, you would probably record most of the major areas of similarity.

Both the talk and the reading are acts of oral communication. Each talk and reading is concerned with the delivery of an idea—an "idea" being an item of information, mood, thought, description, or any other facet of the content. Here are other areas of similarity:

1. Your delivery entails good vocal production (breathing, phonation, resonance, articulation and pronunciation); vocal expression (pitch, volume, rate, and quality); and physical

1

expression (posture, animation, and movement);

2. You respond to your materials; your audience hears and sees, and comprehends; your audience reacts; and you re-pond to your audience;

3. A healthy attitude is maintained throughout.

Vocal Production

Breathing, phonation, resonance, articulation, and pronunciation are basic to the production of recognizable sounds.

Breathing is to the voice what electricity is to the phonograph—the power. Air passes through the larynx and vibrates the vocal folds, thus producing a sound. Relaxed, abdominal breathing is best for a talk or reading. Thoracic, or chest, breathing can pro-duce an ample quantity of air, of course, but just before you speak, the abdominal muscles must be activated for control of the air. This transfer of muscle activity from the thorax to the abdomen can produce tension and a surge of air when the breath is first re-leased. With abdominal breathing, your control is already there, since the abdominal muscles are in motion and require little effort for facile operation. In addition, abdominal breathing is scarcely noticeable to your listeners, whereas chest breathing can be more than a little distracting. Of course, chest breathing may be preferred for a certain effect, such as a sigh which might help to express ela-tion or melancholy.

The next phase of vocal production is phonation. You may have heard nostalgic references made to the aeolian harp, a box and string instrument which was seen on many window sills at the turn of the century. When a breeze passes over the aeolian harp, the strings gently vibrate, and a musical tone is produced. In the larynx, air passes between two membranous tissues known as the vocal cords. More properly, these are vocal folds, which may be stretched wide or narrow at will. The vocal folds are operated by a network of muscles, which control the shape and size of the open-ing between the folds. The vocal folds vibrate gently or rapidly, depending upon the stream of air, and produce a sound. The sound produced is less audible than the sound of a phonograph when the volume is nearly off.

Resonance amplifies the sound. The upper part of the thorax, the throat, mouth, nose, and sinuses comprise the main resonators, which are the amplifying chambers. The size and shape of the resonators largely determine the sound of the voice, and since no two people possess resonators which are identical in size and shape, no two voices are exactly alike. Your voice sounds differently when you have a cold, for the size and shape of the resonators are altered by the infection. A nasal effect is readily produced when the resonance is altered. And the widespread imitations of James Cagney and other performers are evidence of our ability to change the size and shape of the resonators with relative ease.

Articulation and pronunciation are terms which are sometimes used interchangeably. Let's restrict their meanings in this way:

Articulation regards the shaping of the sounds into coherent utterances (syllables). The lips, teeth, tongue, cheeks, and roof of the mouth (hard and soft palates) are the tools of articulation. Since these tools were intended for eating—speech, developed by man, is a secondary function—it is not too surprising that it takes the first four years of our lives to learn to control them for speaking purposes. Observe the tongue, that writhing mass of muscle which is the devil to subdue as you watch it in a mirror, and you have a notion of the tremendous accomplishment you made years ago in learning to speak coherently.

Pronunciation also regards the correctness of the sounds produced, and in addition, is concerned with the stressing and arranging of the syllables into more meaningful sounds (words). As an example, A-NÍ-MAL might be articulated well, but would be dreadful pronunciation, since the accent has fallen on the wrong syllable.

A brief look at two other terms may be helpful. *Enunciation* is generally mentioned with regard to robust and distinct articulation. *Diction,* the overlord of articulation, pronunciation, and enunciation, includes the meanings of all three terms, even extending into the style of expression and choice of words spoken.

Vocal Expression

While vocal production is closely allied to vocal expression—for example, incorrect pronunciation expresses something in itself—the elements of vocal expression normally function after the production of recognizable sounds: pitch, volume, rate, and quality.

The pitch of a voice is determined by the position of the larynx in the throat. Notice the position of a young man's adam's apple, which is part of the larynx. When the adam's apple is high in the throat, his voice is high. His voice is high because the sound waves have a higher frequency in a shortened throat-column. When the larynx is positioned low in the throat, the pitch is low. The pitch is very expressive. When one screams hysterically, for example, the pitch is extremely high—and quite expressive.

The volume is determined largely by the amount of air released from the lungs. A speaker needs to be heard by the person sitting in the back row, and although voice quality and crisp articulation can aid voice projection immensely, volume remains a major consideration. Of course, the use of microphones has almost eliminated need for great volume in a number of speaking situations. Even more important than audibility is the *precise level* of volume needed for expression of various parts of the talk or reading. The young man, for example, who wins his love by shouting sweet nothings in her ear is a rare individual.

When we become excited about something, our rate of speech increases naturally. We are so anxious to share the experience or idea that we attempt to get it across as quickly as we can. You may notice that a person's first talks and readings may be spoken too rapidly, out of the excitement resulting from a speaking situation which is new to him. A conscious effort to speak slowly may prove invaluable, especially in the early part of the talk or reading. Also, in time, you will discover that light material can be communicated more rapidly than matter of a more serious nature, since serious material demands a little more time for the cerebral activities of the audience.

Another element of vocal expression is quality. Strictly speaking, quality is the character, or essential nature, of the voice. Quality should not be confused with the pitch or volume of a sound, however, for at any given pitch and volume the quality of the voice may be either harsh or melodious. To a singer, quality means something of a little different nature. A singer with a breathy, soft voice is said to possess little vocal quality.

A singer produces a tone, which is a sound pleasing to the ear and the opposite of noise. (This last statement may produce some confusion in the minds of those who have grown up quite accustomed to the vocal gymnastics of certain popular singing sensations.) Quality is also affected by the attitudinal tone ("suspicious tone," "joyful tone," etc.) and by the presence of vocal energy. While some individuals seem intent on developing a rapturous, mesmerizing quality, we are after a vocal quality that is *first and foremost expressive*.

In passing, it should be mentioned that the pause, or absence of vocal sound, is also highly expressive, and deserving of further attention in the following chapter.

Physical Expression

The effective speaker or reader knows the value of posture. Normally a speaker is at ease and natural, allowing some of his personality to come through his talk. Ironically, he finds that he is the most relaxed when he stands somewhat alert, with his weight distributed evenly on his feet. The even distribution of weight on both feet has a calming effect on the speaker. It makes him feel comfortably anchored, and more in command of himself and his material. The shifting of weight from foot to foot is actually tiring and emotionally disturbing for the speaker, distracting for his audience. Also, the sling-hip stance belies a speaker's interest in his talk. And to play flamingo by wrapping one leg around the calf of the other and thereby being forced to lean upon the speaker's stand—leave that to the flamingo, who must do something to compensate for his lack of speech.

All speakers and readers are animated, to greater and lesser degrees, depending upon the material, the size of the room or theatre, and vitality of the speaker, among other things. The free-and-easy tone of conversational speaking heard today calls for spontaneity in gestures. A movement of the hand or arm, a lifting or lowering of the chin, a jutting forward of the head—these and other moments of animation are used in conjunction with the spoken word, and are most effective when they seem unpremeditated, or spontaneous. Gestures are used to emphasize a point, to suggest a mood or image, and generally to signal to the listeners that the material is significant. Facial expressions are of exceptional value, particularly when the audience can readily observe your face, and the eyes have a good deal to say, with their gaiety or sadness. Eye contact is normal in conversation, invaluable in speaking and reading.

Most speakers and readers do not move from place to place very much. Some speakers take a step or two to introduce a new point in their material, and a few pace a bit in order to unroll their talk for the audience, but most of us remain in a more or less fixed location. Certainly there is no rule on the number and size of the steps a speaker is allowed per minute. I would suggest that you take few steps until you learn how the audience reacts to your movements.

A lecturer was once speaking in the area between the front row and the stage of a theatre. He moved from one side of the area to the other. In the center of the area was a one-foot drop, which was the landing of the steps leading to the space below the stage. After a half an hour of bobbing up and down across the center area, he must have sensed the anxiety he was stirring in his audience each time he approached the pit without looking, for he stopped and said, "I hope my walking doesn't bother you." The audience laughed heartily, and their tensions were relieved. Movement can be a good thing, if it does not run away with you.

Response and Reaction

Perhaps you have already discovered that the reactions of the audience begin at the speaker's stand; that is, that the speaker can guide the reactions of the audience to an appreciable extent. He may speak in an agreeable way, and the listeners will respond with good will. Later he may alter his approach to an intense, hushed tone, and the audience will normally become serious and extremely attentive, since his tone has signalled that what he is saying is quite meaningful.

In order to get the desired reaction, the speaker responds to his material. If the material is humorous, he tells and shows the audience it is humorous by using light, airy vocal and physical expressions. Except in the case of satire perhaps, the opposite approach would be true for more serious material, the speaker being somewhat more somber. Whatever the nature of the material in a talk or reading, the effective speaker or reader is *in tune with his material,* changing his tone and expressions with the variations of the material.

The audience's response to the spoken word is the result of an interesting process. A word is spoken, and the sound of the word travels through the air in minute vibrations, or sound waves. The sound waves strike the ear, and a message is relayed by a network of nerve fibres extending from the inner-ear to a part of the brain which has recorded our experience with audio sensations. By a succession of instantaneous relays of the message within the brain, we hear.

The brain stores a memory of sounds, and unless the sound-message received in the brain creates an emotional or mental disturbance, perhaps by association with an unpleasant experience, the sound-message is transformed into a meaningful image in the listener's mind. Of course, a person comprehends only those words whose meanings are known to him, and unfamiliar words are likely to bring about confusion. The meaning of the word "enjoin," for example, may not be known to all members of an audience, and since the sound of the word does not suggest the meaning of the word, momentary confusion could result. Whether or not you would use a great number of such words in a talk depends upon your function as a speaker, and you would have to formulate your purpose: Are you trying to expand the audience's vocabulary or establish immediate communication?

When your audience responds openly, either by laughing, nodding approval, or sitting quietly with serious looks and rapt atten-

tion, it is fairly easy for the inexperienced speaker or reader to respond to their reactions and continue the talk or reading with vitality. When listeners do not express their response so noticeably, the
inexperienced speaker may think the listeners are indifferent, and
thus lose heart. After a few talks and readings, you will come to
realize that listeners do not always laugh (or even smile) at everything that is humorous to them; listeners do not always nod in
agreement with you, even though they may be profoundly in agreement; and listeners do not always check their gaze from straying
occasionally to a flower or window, even though they may be
deeply moved by the talk or reading.[1] They are curious people,
these listeners, and Chapter Four is given to a study of their
traits.

When listeners are not responding openly as you had hoped, and
perhaps envisioned, it's best to keep any dismay from being heard
and seen in the talk or reading. If anything, continue with renewed
energy, rather than lessen your effort. Much the best course is to
continue responding to your materials with sustained vitality. Such
a practice will result in a talk or reading that is more gratifying for
you, and more interesting to the audience, than if you had "given
in to the arguments of defeat" and rushed on in order to spare
yourself effort and embarrassment. You spare yourself embarrassment by making an effort.

Incidentally, it is good to respond to unforeseen incidents that
draw the attention of the entire audience. In her first performance,
a young actress was about to make her entrance through a door
when the door frame came loose from the stage setting and pitched
forward onto the stage floor. Although the young lady was startled
for a moment, she evidently remembered that "the show must go
on." She proceeded to step over the door and continue the scene.
The leading man, who realized that this was a time when the show
must not go on, returned the door to its rightful place, and before
continuing with the scene, he smiled and said to the girl, "The door
fell." Much to the delight of the audience, who had become un-

---

[1] Don't be alarmed to find a few of your peers looking about the audience
at times. An industrious student sitting in the audience may occasionally
gauge reactions for his own future reference.

nerved not only by the accident but also by the girl's disregard of a door lying in her living room.

No one can simply ignore a disaster. Should something unforeseen occur, I suggest that you neither collapse, quit, nor curse, but offer some remark in passing. The audience will understand.

The Right Attitude

A healthy attitude is as important to the reader as it is to the speaker. I recall a young English major who got off on the wrong foot with his first reading. His introduction to the reading went something like this: "You are about to hear T. S. Eliot's 'Preludes'. And if you haven't heard it before, I don't know what you're doing in college." The young man then read "Preludes" in the icy arena which he had created. His classmates might have enjoyed the reading if they had not been provoked in so flagrant a manner. As it occurred, their sensibility had been cauterized for the moment.

There is nothing gladitorial in the speaking and reading situations, of course. A reader, for example, is not being set up against a group of people when he stands before them. He is asked to introduce his audience to an experience with the material he has prepared, and his audience is hopeful that he will do a good job of making the material meaningful. The audience in a speech class, moreover, is decidedly *for* the reader, since the class members much prefer an enlivened and enjoyable experience to an unrewarding experience. The classroom audience is similar to nearly all audiences in that the listeners are on the side of the reader, and are hopeful he will do well.

Realizing that the audience is with you is the first step in developing a healthy attitude toward talking or reading to a group. The next step is actually the result of having the right attitude: the reader's offering those courtesies normally extended to people he's meeting for the first time. By being civil, agreeable, and interested in the people, the reader will discover the amiable and responsive nature of the audience. And this relation with an audience is fuel for the right attitude toward future speaking and reading experiences.

DISSIMILARITIES IN THE TALK AND READING

A talk and a reading are similar in many ways, as the earlier part of this chapter attempts to show. There are basic differences between the two, of course, and these points of dissimilarity are the concern of the remainder of the chapter. We begin now to focus more attention on the nature of reading aloud.

Speech Composition and the Printed Page

A talk is something spoken, and is seldomly read from a paper. At times the talk *is* read from a prepared text, but usually only when exact wording is imperative, such as in a major address to the United Nations. Since your talk with a group is on a more local level, and probably not in the nature of a major public address, an attempt to get exact wording prepared in advance is not as important as the attempt to communicate directly during the talk.

Perhaps you are already in the habit of writing, or composing, your talks. A "written talk" would seem to be a contradiction of terms, since writing and talking are two independent avenues of communication. Indeed, when a written talk is read poorly, the contradiction of terms is there for all to behold. This is not to say that written talks cannot be effective at times, but it is apparent that audiences most often prefer the engaging extemporaneous talk to the better formulated, but less spontaneous, written talk.

Obviously, the reading aloud of a printed page of material will also have to be spontaneous. In numerous cases, the reader seeks that enlarged conversational tone which is normally heard in talks. If the reader is to achieve a natural and unstilted sound in his oral expression, he must do so with words which are not his own. And in this matter, the reader differs appreciably from the speaker, who holds the advantage of talking with a rhythm of speech that is naturally and entirely his own.

The reader works with what is written—hopefully, well written. His words are prepared for him; they are fixed in printer's ink. He studies and works with the written material, but except for an introduction to his reading, he is not asked to supply words of his own. In working with his material—the reader spends as much time in preparation as the speaker, and sometimes more—the reader may find that the writing is not always comfortable to speak, not in agreement with his natural oral expression. The sentence construction may be awkward for him at first, stiff and unnatural. This is understandable, for the writer communicates through the written word, and does not always concern himself with the sound of the writing.

Of two recent American writers, Faulkner and Hemingway, many readers will find Hemingway more "conversational" than Faulkner, since the latter writer occasionally turns clause upon clause in a lengthy sentence, creating a rich mosaic of description or narration. It is the reader's part, then, to become so familiar with the author's style that he can speak the written words as if they were his own.

Sentence structure; rhythm; dialogue, in drama and some narratives; and rhyme and meter, in *some* poetry; these are but a few items which may at times distinguish the sound of a writing from the sound of a talk.

The Collaboration of Reader and Writer

In a talk, a person speaks his own thoughts and feelings. The reader, on the other hand, speaks from a writing, which reflects the mind and heart of a writer. In his role as a communicator, the reader is more removed from the audience than the speaker. The reader's communication with the audience is no less real, but it is less direct, since he is something of a medium for another man's thoughts and feelings.

To say that the reader is the mere instrument of the writer would be very misleading, however, for the writing is totally dependent upon the reader for its oral expression. Moreover, when a reader is casting about, searching for the right material to read to his group, the author must vie with every writer in history, living or dead, and the matter of his being selected is entirely at the discretion of the reader. So the reader is very much at the helm.

The reader being given such omnipotence, would it be too paradoxical to say that, following the reader's performance, the audience should be more impressed with the writing than the reader? If so, the matter must be accepted as one of those hard ironies of omnipotence, for once the reader selects his material, he becomes a selfless interpreter of the author's work. That the reader becomes "selfless" means that he is more concerned with his interpretation of the material than with a display of his personality and intellect. He puts the writing first.

Reading Aloud and Impersonation

Most of what you will read aloud requires little impersonation, or suggestion of character. The classroom essay uses no dialogue as a rule, and except for an occasional smear of coffee or red ink, the treasurer's report has no character.

Many prose and poetry selections are narratives, however, and while there may be little or no dialogue in many cases, the character of the narrator should be suggested if his presence is felt strongly in the writing. Consider the narrator in Sherwood Anderson's "I'm a Fool":

Gee whizz, Gosh amighty, the nice hickory-nut and beech-nut and oaks and other kinds of trees along the roads, all brown and red, and the good smells, and Burt singing a song that was called Deep River, and the country girls at the windows of houses and everything. You can stick your colleges up your noses for all me. I guess I know where I got my education.

The boy's language marks him as a character who, although deficient in formal education, finds great joy in his way of life. Since the story is actually an expression of the boy's nature, some suggestion of his character is justified in the reading. You won't be so literal as to chew on a piece of straw or undergo a transformation of your personality, but your vocal and physical expressions are not likely to be as they are ordinarily in a talk.

When Helen Trueblood talks to the members of her literary society each week, there is no mistaking that it is she talking. Mrs. Trueblood is her genial, well-read self, and there is no question of her being anyone else. When the good lady opens a book under discussion—let's say it's *Huckleberry Finn*—and reads a passage of dialogue, a slight change comes over the voice and appearance of Helen Trueblood. She is still Helen Trueblood, as every member of the book club is aware, and yet she is not *quite* herself. She is a brocade version of Huck Finn on a Mississippi raft, or a fashionable rendition of old Aunt Polly. Her mind, emotions, and attitudes reach out to the people in the story, and bring an image of them to the people in the audience. Helen Trueblood remains Helen Trueblood, but she is creating images of other people through her own personality, an act which is called impersonation.

In the above example, the reader's personality did not undergo a change, although some less familiar facets of her personality may have been witnessed by the ladies of the book club. More importantly, the identity of the lady as Helen Trueblood was diminished, and consequently her communication with the audience (as Helen Trueblood) was less direct. Although her own identity will never disappear entirely, the more she enters the character in the reading, the more removed her real identity becomes.

The reader sacrifices some part of his identity to the emotional and intellectual expression required by the material he is reading. Therefore, the degree of directness he has with the audience in a talk is not as great in the reading, although his communication with the audience is no less real in the reading. This "degree of directness" will serve as the basis for one final distinction to be made before you delve into the particulars of reading aloud.

Reading Aloud and Acting

The actor usually has less direct contact with his audience than any other type of oral communicator. This is especially true in realism, the prevailing mode of modern theatre, where the actors speak and gesture to each other and pretend that an audience is not watching and listening to them. The actor's communication with the audience is no less real than the reader's, but it *is* less direct, since the actor must normally be more withdrawn from the audience. In most modern theatre productions, the actor performs *for* the audience, and does not participate *with* the audience as much as the reader does.

The reader is never asked to perform as an actor might for his audience, primarily because he cannot afford to become involved with his material to that degree. When an actor weeps and falls upon the floor, as Romeo does in Friar Lawrence's cell, he is free to give a prolonged expression of his character's anguish. But if a reader weeps and falls upon the floor, what is he to do when he must instantly assume the character of Friar Lawrence and administer advice to the crestfallen Romeo? If he were to get up, dry his tears, and continue reading, one might next see the audience in tears—of laughter.

The actor is normally responsible for only one characterization, which is made more complete by make-up and costume. The reader is at times responsible for many characters, and cannot afford to limit the range of his appearance by wearing a costume. The reader may tug at the lapel of his coat to suggest a mannerism, but his use of costume does not go far. This is not to the disadvantage of the reader, for he has the opportunity to *suggest* more than the actor and can therefore make greater use of the audience's imagination. On the contrary, the reader's access to the imagination of his audience is of infinite value in communicating the varied moods, thoughts, and images found in most reading selections, and is the envy of every actor.

In closing this introduction to reading aloud, it seems suitable to recall what Charles Laughton, an extraordinary actor and reader, felt about his reading experiences:

It is a friendly thing to read from great books. . . . I have always been a nervous actor and scared of appearing before audiences. I have never yet been scared when I have had a bundle of books under my arm.

Your books will become as meaningful to you when you have mastered the following techniques of reading aloud.

Chapter Two

THE READER'S CRAFT

When we were children we were wildly expressive, vocally and physically. In time we learned that such open and vital expression was not the adult way, and we managed to squelch our tendencies toward robust expression. Thus, the *size* of an adult's expressiveness is comparatively much smaller than a child's. This is one of the hazards of maturity.

Let's clear the room of this particular hazard. Of all the things that might dampen the effectiveness of your first few readings, the reserved and cautious, or "mature," approach is probably the best wet blanket for the job. The audience much prefers a reading that is large in size and free in expressiveness to a reading that is rigidly controlled. If you and your classmates will dare to open yourselves to each other, then you will have the courage to be good in reading aloud.

Therefore, a consideration which underlies all the matters to be discussed in this chapter should be borne in mind at this time: if you won't let the "winds of emotion" blow, your reader's craft can only be becalmed and lost at sea.

TO BEGIN

The reader's craft consists of the techniques used in reading aloud, and these techniques are the individual ways by which the reading is expressed, vocally and physically. Although techniques are so important that this entire chapter is given to them, they are only means to an end, and that end is meaning.

The intellectual and emotional meaning of a writing is not expressed by techniques alone. The techniques are only meaningful when "the winds blow," when there is conviction in the reading, when the reader is interested in what he reads as well as in how he reads it.

Nonetheless, all readers depend heavily upon techniques to make their points, or express the meaning. Know exactly what is to be done during the reading. Plan and rehearse the techniques worked out for a particular reading—the techniques will vary from reading to reading—and leave nothing to chance. Although technique is not the be-all and end-all of good reading, it is the beginning of all effective reading aloud.

Although vocal and physical techniques are closely related during the process of reading aloud, it is best to consider them separately for the moment. Later on, we will consider the two together.

USE OF THE BODY

A Chinese opera director attended a performance at the Metropolitan Opera, and following the performance, commented that the movements of the leading soprano weren't effective. His companion concurred, and mentioned an ineffective gesture of farewell the soprano had made with her right hand. The opera director asked his companion how it might have been better, and the reply came that the gesture should have come from the shoulder. "Yes," the opera director said, "if you mean the *left* shoulder."

The difference betweeen reading aloud and singing (and acting) in an opera is one of degree, for both are interpretative by nature. Although you will not likely read in a room as vast as an opera house, physical expressions must still be complete and motivated. In addition, physical expressions will have emphasis, appropriateness, definition, and suggestiveness, topics which will be described in the next few pages.

Physical Techniques

Physical techniques are often used to emphasize significant parts of the reading. The body might be held firm and erect, when reading a passage describing a Victorian mansion, to suggest the stern morality of the late nineteenth century. The eyes might take on a softer look in reading about an idyllic countryside. The index finger might be raised and waggled (not too vigorously, please) to suggest a pompous parliamentarian proclaiming his daily dose of nonsense.

The possibilities for different physical techniques are almost endless, and a little imagination will help to enrich each of your readings with meaningful gestures and physical attitudes. Of course, the physical techniques used will be determined by the points you are trying to make in the reading.

This is a way of saying that the physical techniques should be appropriate to the written material, and thereby express something which is in the writing. Consider the stance of the military officer who reads the sentence of execution to a man facing the firing squad. Standing at attention, the officer's physical attitude is appropriate since it suggests authority, discipline, and the unrelenting nature of a code of justice.

The technique should not only be appropriate to the meaning of the writing, it should also be appropriate to the size of the room. A gesture which is appropriate in an auditorium may be too large for a classroom. When the gesture is too large, attention is drawn to it, and consequently the words do not register as well with the audience. But again, don't be reluctant to be generous with your expression until you learn the quantity and size of expression that is good for your reading style.

Each physical expression should also be definite. This is not to say that each gesture needs to be Forceful and Dynamic. On the contrary, a head movement suggesting an indecisive, henpecked husband might be rather weak and vague. But the expression should always be a definite communication of *something* to the audience, and should have definition in its form. If your posture is to suggest pride, for example, practice until you suggest pride without showing any trace of arrogance, stubbornness, or other extraneous attitudes. Being precise in your techniques—and it takes work!—is a matter of importance if you want to be effective.

We come to a word which has been referred to repeatedly thus far: suggest. Physical expressions should be used to *suggest,* and not fully illustrate, the point the reader is trying to make. Through his physical suggestions, the reader can bring into play one of the most powerful elements in communication—the audience's imagination. The image of a spreading chestnut tree can be created more effectively by the audience's imagination than by a reader's gestures. No fluttering fingertips, descending from overhead, can create a picture of snow falling as well as the audience's imagination.

When the selection contains an image which the audience can readily picture, avoid overt gestures. For example, when the snow starts falling, it's best not to jog from foot to foot to show that you're trying to keep warm, or to turn up your collar against the back of your neck. You *could* pull your arms closer to your side—slowly, imperceptively—continue reading, and let the imagination of your audience do the rest.[1] Since the audience brings a wealth of experience to the reading, you can be sure that everyone will envision a snowfall differently. And rather than satisfy one and perhaps disappoint twenty with an enactment of snow falling, you will fire the imagination of the entire audience.

Special attention is due to the hands. The hands should also be suggestive, rather than descriptive. Occasionally in literature you will find descriptions of a person holding his head in his hands, or someone wringing his hands, or still another person wiping his brow. The reader will almost never perform these actions.

The actions are performed by the characters for definite reasons. Find out the reasons—in the above cases, perhaps they were sorrow, nervousness, and hot weather, respectively—and suggest the reasons physically. It is possible to suggest surprise, for example, with your hands, but more than likely you will be most effective with a subtle facial expression.

The Technique That Sees

Most of the time the audience will get a subliminal impression from the physical expressions, subliminal because the audience is

---

[1] It would be narrow of me to recommend this technique for every story that describes a snowfall. Some snowfalls are exhilarating; some simply freezing. I cite the above technique, and others throughout the book, with a realization that many different techniques could be used for a given situation.

not always watching the toss of the shoulder, the lift of the head. The audience is often looking into the reader's eyes. This behooves the reader to work sedulously for effective eye communication. And what applies to eye technique might well be said with reference to all techniques, physical and vocal: *the expression comes from inside.*

In a very real sense, the eyes are the windows through which the audience sees the reader's feelings and ideas. When we are happy, the eyes glisten and have a light of their own. When we are bored, the eyes are equally telling. One thing certain can be said of eye communication in relation to reading aloud. If you have prepared the reading so thoroughly that you can recall your first reactions to the writing while reading to the audience, it is likely that your eye communication will be effective. If the preparation has been slight, the eyes will tell.

Of course, there is a unique dimension in eye communication for the reader. He must look to the audience, and yet return to the writing from time to time. Most of his attention will go to the audience, and a good understanding of the writing will enable the reader to move from the writing to the audience, and back again, with relative ease. As in speaking, don't try to sweep the entire audience each time you look up. Look at a few people at a time, focusing upon one person at a time, and, it is hoped, you will have looked at and read to everyone by the time the reading has ended.

The smaller the group the more vital is the need for eye contact. The intensity of the eye communication will be decreased for smaller groups, but the need for eye contact is nonetheless real. In addition, the eyebrows should be passive for small groups, just as the TV newscaster's eyebrows are normally passive. The eyebrows and forehead are restricted with small groups and on the TV screen because at such close range the degree of the eyebrows' animation would detract from the vocal communication.

There are a few times when you will communicate best by making little or no eye contact at all. When the material is very intimate—as in certain lyric poems, dramas, and works of fiction—the eye contact may make your communication too personal, as if the intimate thought were being expressed by you and not the author. Occasions for restricting your eye contact will be rare enough, however, and until you are sure that eye contact should be restricted for a particular selection, look to the audience and let the people see what you are saying.

USE OF THE VOICE

A reader does not need a musical, resonant voice in order to be effective. What the reader does need are (1) a determination to use his voice's potential and (2) an understanding of vocal techniques.

Your Voice Potential

At one time or another in your life your voice has expressed every emotion and feeling: grief, joy, confusion, anger, elation, curiosity, suspicion. In fact, you may need voice training much less than you need the awareness of a basic truth: you are capable of expressing the full range of human experience right now. If you have vocally expressed joy in the past, you can do it again, because you have also experienced a feeling called determination.

Knowing that your voice is capable of the most subtle expressions is the first step. The second step is the past. That is, by rekindling the emotional experiences in your past *while you are reading to the audience,* your reading will communicate more effectively. This is the process of sense-recall, which will be described a bit later in the chapter. Suffice it to say at this point that your voice is capable of answering almost any command you can give it, and its usefulness, its effectiveness—as we might naturally have suspected —depends upon you.

The Vocal Techniques

There is no definite number of vocal techniques. They are legion. You will find some more useful than others, and the more useful ones may be used repeatedly. Moreover, each reading presents you with new possibilities. Let's consider some of the vocal techniques by categories: rate, pitch, volume, and quality.

When reading a story that has several different characters in it, give some thought to the rate of each character's speech. As you know, some people talk faster than others, and the rhythms of speech differ from person to person. It would be illogical then to always assume that four different characters in a given story or play would have the same rate of speech. Regarding characterization, we associate a fairly rapid rate of speech with an excitable or vital person, and a slow, easy rate is often the mark of a more relaxed and calm person. Different rates of speech, then, can help you to distinguish between multiple characters in a story.

Even more frequently, rate can be used to set off important points in the reading. You will find it only too easy to "run over" your points by reading too fast. (Forewarned is forearmed.) By slowing up when reading a part that is quite significant, you will be signaling its significance to the audience, and you are assured of added attention. You can speed up on parts that are less significant, parts that require relatively little cerebral activity or emotional reaction of the audience.

If you speed up and slow down at the right places, you are accomplishing two things of importance: (1) You're putting the parts in their proper order of significance, thereby making the writing more meaningful for the audience, and (2) you're giving your reading variety.

The pitch of the reader's voice deserves special attention. When reading aloud we seldomly depart from our normal pitch for an appreciable length of time. However, we do raise and lower the pitch, and we do it for definite reasons, some of which are cited below:

1. To signal that we are beginning a new part of the reading: Raising the pitch.
2. To signal that we are ending a part of the reading: Lowering the pitch.
3. To suggest a character's extreme emotional state: Raising the pitch.
4. To arouse suspense: Lowering the pitch.
5. To emphasize, or set off, a point: Raising or lowering the pitch.

Actually, not one of these random examples is absolutely valid. In each of the first four examples, the pitch may have been raised or lowered with equal effectiveness, depending upon the reader. In the fifth example, the pitch might have continued in its normal pattern. The criteria for selecting techniques involving pitch are the appropriateness of the technique to the writing and the suitability of the technique to the reader's voice.

The overall volume level of a particular reading will depend upon a number of factors: the size of the room and audience; the nature of the writing; the colors in the background of the reader; and the condition of the weather, among myriad other considerations. The most important of these considerations are the size of the room and the nature of the writing, the latter being nearly always *the* most important.

If the writing is a vitriolic indictment of injustice, the volume is likely to be high overall. When the writing is more passive, the volume is usually lower. The specific volume levels used during the reading will depend upon the developments within the writing.

Few indictments-of-injustice roll on at fever pitch without some reflective comments or humorous asides. The reader will be responsive to such changes of tone in the writing, and by lowering the volume, give the audience an occasional relief the author has provided in his writing.

As in other aspects of technique, volume can be used to emphasize the more significant parts of a writing. Should you find a sentence or whole paragraph that represents the theme or a major item of interest in the writing, increase the volume for it. There may be many significant parts in a writing, and in such a case, you would increase the volume for each part. The opposite technique —decreasing the volume for significant parts—can be used occasionally with equal success.

When reading a selection which has dialogue, consider the volume suitable for each character, just as you would consider the rate of each character's speech. A brash individual is likely to be loud, a more introverted individual quiet. Such characters, "brash" and "introverted," are stereotypes, of course, and much can be said in defense of presenting them as such, for stereotypes communicate instantly to the audience.

The remaining area of vocal expression, quality, has several applications in reading aloud. If the purpose of the writing is to incite the audience to action, a harsh and muscular vocal quality might be best. If the selection is lyric poetry, a softer, more agreeable quality would be appropriate. Again, the selection of the technique depends upon the nature of the writing.

When the author satirizes his subject, will your vocal quality also pooh-pooh the subject? Or will your vocal quality, or tone, imply that the author is serious in his treatment, leaving the communication of the satire to the words? Both approaches are valid, the former being the more common of the two.

Although the matter of quality is generally less significant than the techniques of rate and volume, the quality for a given reading should be decided upon and practiced until the right effect is achieved.

The Technique That Is Silent

If given the attention it deserves, one non-vocal tcehnique which will greatly enhance your reading is the pause. Many readers are deaf to the value of this little bit of silence. And yet, more audiences have been won by the effective use of the pause than by the use of any other single technique.

First of all, the reader pauses before he begins the reading. This gives the audience a moment to settle, and indicates that the reading will begin when everyone is ready to give the reader his attention. Also, the reader can use this moment to bolster his determination to do his best.

The pause is invaluable in "breaking up" a reading. By pausing between paragraphs, between sentences, and within sentences, so long as the pause is meaningful, a long reading is made short. In fact, there is no such thing as a "long reading," but merely a series of short readings, when the pause is used effectively.

You can make your points more emphatic with the pause. By pausing before a significant word, phrase, or sentence, you signal to the audience that what follows is important, and the audience is quick to catch the signal. Likewise, by pausing *after* a word, phrase, or sentence, you help the audience to grasp the meaning of what was said.

Pause, if the audience wants to laugh. Whether or not you have anticipated the laugh, let the audience laugh it out. You may recall the frustration of trying to hear an amateur actor who continued to speak while the audience was still laughing. The frustration is no less real when it occurs during a reading. Pause, relax, and breathe.

Often the pause can be used in conjunction with other techniques, and this correlation of vocal and physical techniques in reading aloud is our next concern.

MORE ON TECHNIQUE

I recall a young car salesman who was demonstrating the heating controls in a new car. He had memorized a spiel about the flexibility of the controls, and was pushing buttons and sliding levers all the while he was talking. He lost the sale primarily, I believe, because his technique was shoddy. If he had described the function of the gadget, paused for an instant, then punched the button, his take-home pay could have increased sharply.

Regarding this correlation and timing of physical and vocal techniques, consider a remark from Stephen Leacock's *Model Memoirs:* "It's the women who have made our college life the bright, happy thing it is—too bright, too happy."

Whether or not you agree with the observation, try reading it aloud in several different ways:

1. When do you pause? After "women"? After "thing it is"? After both?
2. Would you look up from the writing on "women"? Would your eyes return to the writing once you have looked up?
3. Would you look up while you are actually reading? Or during the pause(s)?
4. Would you read the first part of the remark as if it were a complete thought, and then add "too bright, too happy"?
5. Can you leave out the pause which the dash seems to call for?

Since the observation is taken out of its context, and therefore may mean more than is apparent here, it's impossible to determine an exact method of reading the sentence. But the briefest analysis reveals that Leacock is saying "women" have made college life "too bright, too happy," and your techniques should help to point this out. In addition, the correlation and timing of your vocal and physical techniques should point up Leacock's humor, however damning it may be in this instance.

One last word on the simultaneous use of vocal and physical techniques. In ordinary conversation we nod our heads, point our fingers, etc., to emphasize certain ideas while we are talking. While reading aloud you will nod or lift your head for emphasis, just as you do in conversation. However, you are justified at times in not using vocal and physical techniques simultaneously.

The audience's attention is divided between sight and sound. When you are reading, a facial expression does not register as well as it would if you were not reading for that instant. Conversely, when you make a facial expression while reading, the words do not register as vividly with the audience. (This is all well and good, since the presence of facial expressions more than compensates for the loss in vocal communication, and vice versa.) Therefore, for some few, very significant, well-worded parts of the reading, speak without any physical expressions in motion. Raise your head, pause, and without moving a muscle other than those necessary for talking, read the writing with full vocal expression. This technique puts all the emphasis on the words spoken, and as a technique, it has been used for centuries by thousands of effective readers.

CRAFT IN PERFORMANCE

Although the actual steps of preparation for a reading will be described in Chapter Three, a matter related to preparation and performance is pertinent at this point: spontaneity.

Gordon Craig, a controversial figure in the early twentieth century theatre, once advocated the use of super-marionettes to replace actors onstage. Craig averred that "art arrives only by design," and since an actor's expression is "at the mercy of the winds of his emotions," actors are imperfect artists. The more perfect artist would be the marionette operator, who could consistently express human emotions scientifically, mechanically. However valid Craig's theory, the rare use of super-marionettes attests to the world-wide preference for live actors, poor creatures that they are.

One of the reasons for the actors' dominance over marionettes is spontaneity, the natural and lively flow of expression. An actor may rehearse a gesture or vocal subtlety a hundred times, and yet give the impression in performance that he is doing it for the first time. Such an actor has spontaneity.

This spontaneity comes from inside the person, and the reader can sometimes aid the spontaneity of his reading with sense-recall, or emotional memory. For writings that have considerable emotional content, the concentration on specific incidents in the reader's past can help to express the emotion in the writing. For example, remembering (just for an instant!) the love you had for a childhood pet can help to express the sorrow reflected in a story which you are reading.

The function of spontaneity is to give the appearance that no techniques have been planned for the reading, even though they may have been planned to the last letter of the writing. If the reader plans all his facial expressions, pauses, etc., and the readings seem "canned" time after time, that reader would be wise to try a different approach. Although "the winds" can blow well enough within the framework of planned techniques—just as some poets write best in a set form, such as the sonnet—some readers may feel constrained by a thorough planning of techniques, and should draw a compromise, concentrating more on what the author is saying and less on the techniques for saying it.

Eventually, you may be able to read aloud without being conscious of the techniques which you are using. But for now, try out many varied techniques whenever you read aloud, techniques which you find appropriate for the writing. True, you are learning techniques in order to forget them—learning techniques so they may be used subconsciously in future readings—but you will first want to become thoroughly familiar with them.

If at first you find yourself carrying out the mechanics but not the spirit of the techniques, and therefore feel and sound a bit wooden, you are perfectly normal, and there is hope for you.

Chapter Three

UNDERSTANDING THE AUTHOR—ALOUD!

A point worth repeating is that technique, or craft, is a means to an end. That "end" is meaning. The reader who relies entirely upon his craft, and doesn't make the effort to understand the author's meaning, is flying a kite into his own head wind. The going is pretty skittish.

The preparation for a reading enables you to make your best possible delivery of the author's writing. The more thorough and productive the preparation, the more assured you are of a good reading.

In the process of preparing the reading, another function is fulfilled. You get to know your material through the analysis and practice readings, and this matter—the development of your understanding of the author's writing—will receive special attention in the pages that follow.

STEPS OF PREPARATION

Before looking into the preparation of a reading, some thought should be given to selecting the writing. It can be a mistake to select a writing because you have heard or read that you *should* like it. Select a writing that you have enjoyed, a work which you believe the audience could also appreciate. Since you will be studying the selection at some length in your preparation, you should feel that the selection is worthy of your time, as well as the audience's. Special occasions may require specialized material, and, obviously, an audience with a special interest (e.g., a club meeting) may need special consideration.

But since the people enrolled in the course you are now studying have such a wide range of interests, the full mosaic of prose and poetry are at your disposal. You may have some difficulty in finally deciding upon a selection, but you will have no trouble in finding writing that has appeal and insight.

If you select only a part of a work, be certain that you have read the entire work before beginning your preparation. The excerpt is a part of the entire work's meaning, and the meaning of the excerpt will be affected by what the rest of the work has to say.

Copying The Selection

For the first few readings, whenever a copy of the writing is permitted and is just as effective to the audience as the original publication, type out the selection which you will read from a reader's stand. Why copy the selection? Because you become more familiar with the author's style and develop a better understanding of what the writing is. Because you will then have a manuscript on which you can make notes and erasures. Because a typed copy is easier to read from than most printed pages. By the way, a typed copy is more functional than a hand-written copy, since any notes made on the pages would appear in your own handwriting and might be confused with the author's writing.

Here are a few specific considerations:

1. Use white paper that has little gloss, preferrably mimeograph paper;
2. Double-space the type and leave sizeable margins;
3. Copy the selection in a form as similar to the original as possible, keeping the same paragraph indentations, punctuation, capitalization, and the like;
4. If the selection has a relatively large number of paragraphs, type the first word of each paragraph in red. The red words will serve as landmarks for keeping your place during the reading;
5. Since few typewriters can reproduce italics, you will invent a device, perhaps underlining, to remind yourself that italics, or some other special type, were used in the original;

6. Make a carbon copy, in case. And if the carbon copy is bolder and easier to read than the first copy, read from the carbon copy.

If the selection is in a library book, type up the bibliographical information before returning the book to facilitate your recovering the book should you need it for reference. Set the typed pages aside—don't staple them—and check the copy for typing errors at your next opportunity.

The First Readings

Your first reading from the typed copy will be a proofreading. Get a friend to hold the original while you read aloud from your typed copy. This is your first audience for the reading, and ideally the experience will be a relaxed give-and-take of information on quotation marks, commas, and other mechanics of the printed page. If a dash of meaning is added to the session, so much the better.

If time permits during this proofreading, make a note of every word or expression that is unfamiliar, either in its meaning or pronunciation. Before you can proceed with an analysis and practice readings, you should use the dictionary to determine the meanings of unfamiliar terms as they are used by the author. Practice the pronunciation of unfamiliar words until the sound of each word is comfortable and fluid.

Your next reading will be for the purpose of getting at the core of the author's writing, and will give you a foundation for studying the selection. Read the selection, and as you go, concentrate on the effect the writing has on you. What is the writing saying to you? How do you react to the writing? What in the writing makes you react the way you do?

Studying the Selection

The three questions above are broad in their scope, and difficult to answer in any but a broad, general way at this time. By getting into more specific matters, however, you will find sound answers to each of the above questions.

The following questions are not all-inclusive, and not all the questions will apply to every selection. The series of questions is designed to give your analysis a point of departure:

I. What Is the Author's *Main Concern?*

Story: Does he seem primarily concerned with development of the story line?

Character: Does he seem more concerned with the psychology of his characters?

Message: Is he primarily concerned with teaching a lesson, perhaps of a social nature?

Information: Is he writing a detailed description of a particular subject?

Atmosphere: Is he writing to establish a mood, or atmosphere?

Humor: Is he writing with an enjoyment of man's foibles?

Background: If an excerpt, is the writing largely concerned with information on the subject's background, perhaps as prelude to something occurring later in the writing?

Thought: Is the author primarily concerned with an examination of ideas?

Can you see things you'll emphasize vocally and physically in order to point up this "main concern"?

II. What Is the Author's *Attitude?*

Story: Does the story have a sad or buoyant effect, reflecting the author's attitude?

Character: Is the author sympathetic, hostile, or objective toward his character(s)?

Message: Does he seem angry and embittered or calm and rational?

Information: Does he write with a fascination for his subject or in a more perfunctory fashion?

Atmosphere: Is his mood oppressive, eerie, or elating?

Humor: Is his humorous treatment of the subject gentle or biting?

Background: Does he report objectively, or is there a warmth or harshness in his treatment?

Thought: Does he seem to feel obligated to examine the idea, or is he extremely interested and involved?

How will the author's attitude affect your reading? His attitude may be a bit elusive at first glance. However, the author's attitude is implanted in the writing, and since you will want to be in tune with the writing, you had better listen to his music until you are sure that you know the tune.

III. What Is the Author's *Intention?*

Story: Is his story drawn to entertain, enlighten, or teach a lesson?

Character: Does his character portrayal represent Man or a man?

Message: Does his message make a plea for action?

Information: Is the information intended for some application, or is it for your general knowledge?

Atmosphere: Is the mood calculated to win your sympathy for a character or circumstance?

Humor: Is the author ridiculing his subject?

Background: Is his background, or prelude, in ironic contrast with the treatment of the subject later in the writing?

Thought: Does he intend to arrive at a truth or resolution, or is he more interested in a reflective, noncommittal inquiry?

Can you see opportunities for stressing and making clear the author's intention?

When you have arrived at a good understanding of what the author has done in his writing, you will know the satisfaction experienced by the writer Racine, who completed a plot outline that would later become *Phédre* and said, "My work is finished." Developing a good understanding of your selection is almost as rewarding as success of the reading itself.

Your analysis is not so much extra work that you must do in preparation for a reading. On the contrary, the answers to the above questions have a very practical application. Once you have arrived at an answer to any of the questions, think about putting your answer to work: How can I get this point across? Should I read it with vigor? Will a slower rate work? Where will a pause help me to say what I want to say? In this way, you are thinking of meaning in terms of technique, and are moving toward the next step of your preparation—the practice readings.

Reading For Sense

After studying the selection, read the selection aloud, and read slowly. The deeper we drop a plow into the earth, the slower the going. Although the plowing is slower, more earth is being furrowed up. Read aloud slowly, and plow up the meaning. You may stop at times to think about the writing—even to discuss it out loud—and to try out a few different ways to read certain parts. Don't be concerned with the time it takes you to read in this way. Be concerned with getting as much out of the reading as you can.

The next practice reading is approached in much the same way. Read aloud slowly, as before. This time, however, don't stop to ponder an expression or meaning, or to experiment with various parts of the reading. Read the entire selection from beginning to end at about half the rate you would normally read. When you have finished this practice reading, work on the parts which you feel deserve special attention, either because they are significant or in need of further work, before proceeding to the next reading.

The Final Practice Readings

In the above readings you read at about half-speed, taking time to sift the meaning as you read. Two or three such practice readings will put you on solid footing, and in a frame of mind similar to the baseball player who has just swung three heavy bats in the on-deck circle—feeling more competent and confident of doing well.

During the next few days read the selection aloud at a normal rate. Improvise a reader's stand for your practice if you are to use one for the reading, and stand up for all the final practice sessions. Keep your body and mind addressed to the audience. If possible, close the windows in your practice room and read to people passing by your window. Try to communicate with these people, and project the writer's work, which you should be absorbing by now, to the people passing by. To prevent your being evicted from the room, do not shout to the passers-by, but nonetheless extend your will to communicate the full distance.

After a few of these practice readings you will discover many nuances of the author's rhythm and style, and if your practice sessions have been particularly productive, you will find need for refining the work you did during your study of the selection. Continue reading the entire selection at a normal rate during the last few days of practice, and on the final day, dress in clothes similar to the ones you will wear for the reading, in order to feel more at ease during your reading the next day.

During these final practice sessions, keep an eye on the time. If you consistently run over the time limit a bit, make a judicious cutting of the writing rather than speed up the reading and leave out the pauses.[1] By now you are getting the idea that the writing doesn't communicate well if read rapidly or perfunctorily, but needs someone who will take his time in reading and make the writing meaningful.

Even more important, keep an eye on the audience, or rather, keep *with* the audience. Your practice sessions should enable you to talk entire sentences to the audience after seeing a word or phrase on the page. In effect, you will have memorized much of the writing during your practice sessions. It isn't always necessary to intentionally memorize the writing; you can't help but learn the words at the same time you learn what they're saying, during the practice readings. And by learning the meaning of what you are reading, the words come to you more easily, more naturally. During the actual reading, you will be able to spend much of your time speaking to the audience. Two-thirds or more of your reading should be given to the audience, in order to make them feel that what they are hearing is alive and vital—and not just so many words on very dry paper.

For a five-minute reading you should practice from five to six hours, beginning a week before the day your reading is scheduled. Any more than this may cause you to weary of the selection, no matter how good its quality; any less than this may cause the au-

[1] The cutting of a writing is illustrated in Chapter Five.

dience to weary of a reading that is underprepared. Practice aloud. Practice aloud with a will to communicate.

Since your practice readings keep you in constant touch with the book or manuscript from which you're reading, some practical matters concerning the preparation and use of the manuscript should now be investigated.

THE MANUSCRIPT

There is a certain charm about turning pages in a book as you read aloud. I recall a large, personable man reading to a fireside group. His book was tilted upward from his chest as if he were holding a secret. You could tell from the way he measured the weight of the book in his hands that he enjoyed what he was reading. And when he turned a page, it was as if he were opening a new realm of adventure. The experience was magical.

One of the problems in using a book, at least for the first few readings, is the matter of making marginal notes. No one likes to mark up a book. Moreover, the margins in many books aren't large enough for effective note-making. Magazines also have their disadvantages. If you are reading a magazine article, and are holding the magazine in view of the audience, the cover of the magazine could be working against your purpose, for it is often unrelated to the article being read. Also, many magazines are difficult to handle, tend to fold at crucial moments, and contain the most bewildering array of double, triple, and quadruple columns.

Therefore, it has been recommended, whenever a reader's stand is used during your first readings, that you type a copy of your selection, and use this copy for your reading manuscript. After the first few readings you should occasionally get away from the reader's stand, and in fact, read from a book. With experience, you may even find it unnecessary to make any marginal notes whatsoever. But for the moment, let's concentrate on the typed manuscript.

The typed manuscript is similar to the note cards you might use for a talk in that the manuscript is for *your* use and may be marked in any way you like. Double spacing, or even triple spacing at times, will give you ample room for underlining with straight or wiggly lines and dashes. Guide words such as "smile," "most serious part," "s–l–o–w–l–y," "look up," "character with low voice→," "REPEAT slight pause," and other expressions are often marked on the manuscript, usually in the margins. If the reading runs ten minutes or longer, you might find it helpful to keep a running account of your practice time at the top of each sheet. Work out a code, whatever is most meaningful to you. You may discover that numerous guide words, circles, lines, arrows, etc., will keep you too busy during the reading, and make you feel something like an instrument. Although it is desirable to be alert and mentally "rewakened" by marginal notes, it is best to begin your practice readings with few marginal notes and add more notes only as you can accommodate them.

Do not add any marginal notes to the manuscript during the last day of practice. And for the same reason, don't make up a fresh copy of the manuscript the day before the reading. *You want to read from the copy with which you're familiar.* Anything new and fresh is likely to throw you off a bit during the actual reading.

It is not to your advantage to staple the sheets together. Keep the loose sheets in a folder, using a paperclip to prevent their falling out. When you put the manuscript on the reader's stand, remove any paperclips and place the sheets on the right hand side of the stand. As you nearly finish reading each sheet, slide the sheet to the left, so that you have two typed sheets facing you. Transferring your attention from one page to another is simplified since you have two pages in front of you at all times.

UNDERSTANDING THE AUTHOR—ALOUD!

Thus far this chapter has been concerned with studying the selection, practicing the reading, and preparing the manuscript for reading. No one facet of preparation is more important than another. If you practice reading long and hard, but make little attempt to study and get the meaning of the selection, the practice may result in nothing more than a musical patter. Likewise, if you study and develop a good understanding of the selection, but give little time to your practice readings, the reading is likely to fall short in expression.

However, there is one facet of the preparation that deserves some emphasis, by way of exclamation mark: Aloud! Practice aloud. In practicing, read to a person, to a lamp, to a hairbrush or comb (avoid the mirror), but read *aloud.*

On page 29, three questions were asked:

1. What is the writing saying to you?
2. How do you react to the writing?
3. What in the writing makes you react the way you do?

Regarding the first question, the *sound* of a writing says something to you. In a relatively simple way, the sound of the following sentence carries meaning: **The boa crushed his prey.** The word "boa" has a soft sound for so powerful a creature, but the sound does have a muscular ripple. The sound of "crushed" is brutal, and the sound of "prey" provides a short, hard finish to the thought. Rarely will you need to analyze the sounds of words, as above, except when reading certain works of more poetic expression. Often, you need only to hear the words in order to understand them better, for the sounds of our language carry meanings which neither the eye can see nor the mind perceive in silence.

The second question can sometimes test your mettle as a reader. Probably, you will not find it essential to apply the question to every thought and image in the writing, and sometimes your reaction may be so mixed and multiple that arriving at a concise answer is out of the question.

But still, you want to get a certain reaction from the audience, and in order to get the reaction you want, you have to know the reaction you're after. By reading the selection aloud in the early practice readings, and pausing to weigh your reactions as they occur, you will have a better idea of the emotional and intellectual currents in the writing. Don't be content with treading water. Swim with these currents, and read your reactions into the reading as you practice. The audience will respond to the reading when you respond to the writing, but again, you can't expect to respond well without sufficient practice—aloud.

The third question—What in the writing makes you react the way you do?—holds a key to making the writing meaningful as you read aloud. With reason, someone might ask, "How can you 'understand' a description of a countryside, or a piece of humorous writing? What is there to understand? In one, a countryside is described, and in the other, something funny is told. Isn't that enough?" And the answer would be, "Yes, that's enough, if you are willing to settle for it. But chances are the audience will not hear all that is in the writing."

The author may detest the sight of the countryside he is describing, or he may stand in awe of it, or be very much attached to it. Three different attitudes—all read aloud in the same way? Not if the three attitudes are to be made distinct from each other. The humorist may be ridiculing his subject, or parodying another writing, or toying with words and ideas. Three different intentions, each requiring a different and distinctive approach.

In other words, the answer to the third question will cast light on your understanding of the author's writing, for something in those three areas of the analysis—the author's main concern, his attitude, and his intention—makes you react the way you do.

The soundest approach to reading effectively is to put your analysis into action and read your thoughts and feelings into the reading. Your reading will emphasize the author's main concern, reflect his attitude toward the subject, and be faithful to his intention. All of this is possible if you have the will to understand him, and make him understandable, aloud.

Chapter Four

UNDERSTANDING THE AUDIENCE

The audience is a person. This person may be four feet high, forty feet wide, and sixty feet deep, or of greater or lesser dimensions. The size may be on a grand scale or small, but as with all people, the size doesn't matter when we think of the person.

No more typically human person can be found. Although each audience has its own personality—just as every school has its own personality—the audience behaves as a single person. The business executives may be more solemn than the members of a fan club, and the members of the P.T.A. may be more withdrawn than students in assembly. But still, the group reacts as a single person during a reading.

The psychology of the audience is of particular interest to the reader. When a person is surrounded by other people and listening to a reader, his individual traits are influenced somewhat by the character of the audience. Usually an individual member of an audience behaves more in the manner which he feels is socially acceptable. Thus, an office worker in the audience may be embarrassed by a joke that would put him in stitches at the water cooler. And who hasn't seen children giggling to control laughter which Society might scold them for? You may have observed your friends' behavior in classrooms, and noticed how it differs from the times they are not members of an audience.

Generally, as members of an audience, we tend to be more moral, more responsive to ideas, more heroic, more respectful, more forgiving—in short, a little bit more of just about everything. We tend to enlarge our personal traits when we are spectators and listeners. We are drawn out of ourselves for a brief time, and become a person of the most broadly human character, the audience.

Of special interest to the reader is the enlargement of peoples' sensibilities when they become members of an audience. A man might stifle an impulse to cry as he walks down a busy street, and yet this same man may weep openly at a stirring play or motion picture. People are more keenly responsive to emotional stimulation when they are members of an audience. Likewise, they are more responsive to comedy and fantasy. Laughter is infectious in an audience, and regarding fantasy, thousands of adults have been amazed to discover that a reading of a fairy tale can still hold them spellbound.

This discussion has been drawn for two points:

1. The reader thinks of the audience, small or large, as a single person;
2. The reader reacts more openly (emotionally and mentally) than he does ordinarily because the members of the audience are more responsive than they are ordinarily.

How does the reader put this information into practice? Of the two points above, the first is almost a prerequisite for the second. The reader who reminds himself as he begins the reading that his audience is a person, and can be treated as a single person, is in a more responsive attitude than the reader who sees row on row of faces, becomes distracted, and loses sight of his goal. This reader who reminds himself that the audience responds as a single person will find it easier to respond to his materials, easier to start the audience reacting in the direction he desires.

WE RESPOND TO WHAT WE SEE AND HEAR

One more word on responsiveness: the audience needs direction in order to respond as a person. A smile or a devilish glint in the eye are comic signals to the audience, and such signals help to guide the audience's reaction. Reading with some pathos in the voice is a signal in the opposite direction, toward an emotional response from the audience. At times, in reading humorous material, you can signal emotion and make the humor even more evident and effective, by way of contrast.

Whatever signals are used, let the audience know the direction of the writing early in the reading, right away if possible. The audience that knows where it is going is an audience that listens to the reader with anticipation and interest.

TO SEE OURSELVES AS OTHERS SEE US

You are waiting for a reader to take the floor. You see him rise and move toward the front of the room. You see his clothes. You see him take a position and get ready to read. From five to twenty seconds after the reader has been announced or introduced, the reading begins. What you see during the time prior to the reading, and what you see and hear during the reading, makes an impression upon you. What impression would you like to make upon the audience?

A favorable one, of course, but even more pertinent than "favorable" and "unfavorable" impressions are the right and wrong impressions, right and wrong in terms of the author's writing. The sounds we vocalize, the gestures we make, the number of times we look at the manuscript—everything we do and say registers with the audience and transmits meaning, hopefully the same meaning that we want to get across. To take some of the guesswork out of your efforts to impress the audience in the right way, put yourself in their seats and try to see and hear yourself as the audience sees and hears you.

With some apology for the coincidence of quoting from "To a Louse" with reference to the audience, I cite Robert Burns's Scottish wit:

> O wad some Power the giftie gie us
> To see oursels as ithers see us!
> It wad frae mony a blunder free us,
>   An' foolish notion:
> What airs in dress an' gait wad lea'e us,
>   An' ev'n devotion!

Of course, no one can see himself as others see him, but a reader who sees and hears other readers can imagine with some accuracy the way that he looks and sounds. At least he can recall that standing with his weight on one foot looks out of place and that keeping his face buried in the manuscript, he is a monument of ob-
~ity. The more evident failings can be avoided easily or correct-

ed in the first few readings if the reader gives some thought to what the audience sees and hears.

This does not mean that the reader should study the decorum and grace advocated by certain etiquette books. You will benefit more as a reader by studying the adventures of Wiley Post, the pilot and friend of Will Rogers, before approaching Emily Post, or the career of Cornelius Vanderbilt, of railroad fame, before tackling Amy Vanderbilt. As you are aware, a reading doesn't consist of so many pretty poses and niceties of expression. The meaning of a writing can only be sidetracked by a reader's overt concern for a beautiful, resonant voice. The meaning will never get off the ground if the reader is constantly thinking of his appearance.

Still, there are a few technical matters which should always concern the reader, since they hold a strong influence on the audience's responses. Chief among these technical matters is eye contact, a subject which was mentioned earlier and which will be investigated again in later chapters.

TO SEE THE AUDIENCE AS A PERSON

Eye communication is an attitude. If you know your material so well that you can spend most of your time telling the writing to the audience, the eyes will often reflect the right attitude. This is the attitude which says, "The audience is the most important person in this room—not me, not the author. The audience comes first in every consideration except the author's meaning, which can't be compromised. I am reading for the audience's pleasure and benefit, and everything I do is designed to increase that pleasure and further that benefit." I have never known an audience to be anything but grateful for a reader who has had that attitude, and I've never known a reader with that attitude who didn't express it with his eyes.

The right attitude toward the audience creates a bond between the reader and his audience, and makes the members of an audience feel a kinship for each other—not a maudlin or saccharine feeling of Togetherness, but an honest enjoyment of participating together.

A few poems and dramatic sketches were being read one summer evening to an audience in a small outdoor theatre. It began to rain, and everyone ran for cover, readers included. When the downpour stopped, the audience returned to their seats, made arrangements to keep dry, and the readings were resumed. The rain had improved that audience a hundred fold. Everyone had been running around, getting wet, and had shared an experience which fused their interests in the readings.

There was nothing mysterious or mystical about the transformation of the audience's behavior. Before the rain, they were a group of individuals who regarded each other mildly, as if they were all fellow shoppers in a large department store. After participating together in an effort to keep dry, the people were in good spirits on a common ground, and they became an audience, participating in the readings as a single person.

Unfortunately, most readings occur indoors. But still, the reader can do a great deal to put the audience on a common ground. Primarily, he does it with the reading itself. He can also do it with an introduction to the reading. By remarking on aspects of the writing, the author, the reader's experience during his preparation, and other topics related to the audience and the reading, the reader can find material which will draw his particular audience together. Finally, the reader can unite the audience by his attitude and a liberal amount of eye contact, and in so doing, help the audience to see and appreciate what he is saying.

No reader can expect to fully implement his understanding of the audience in his first readings. Somehow some do, and the experience is rewarding for reader and audience alike when it occurs. The best approach toward establishing the right relationship with the audience is to let the audience know you have the right attitude toward them.

When you are honest and respectful with your audience, the audience rewards your attitude by responding as openly as they can. Their response may not be as wildly enthusiastic as you had hoped, but then even the experienced reader cannot hope for a response that is outwardly enthusiastic. The experienced reader knows that the audience is similar to an iceberg in that most of the response will occur below the surface. He also knows that, unlike the iceberg, the audience has a great deal of warmth and heart, and a human quality that can be felt by the reader who works to understand it.

Chapter Five

THE RIGHT INTERPRETATION

We have a novel, and we have a newspaper. One is a work of fiction, and the other journalism. Fiction and journalism communicate to a reader by means of the printed word. They are alike in that. They differ in a number of ways, and while the inky fingers we get from newsprint is the symptom of a most annoying difference, the most significant difference between the two lies in what each communicates. Although generalizations are often misleading and never absolutely true (including the one just stated), we might say that journalism reports life, fiction interprets it.

Traditionally, reading aloud has been associated with literature and not journalism. When a reader reads, he does more than "report life." He reads the selection in such a way that life is re-created, in such a way that the writing affects the audience in the same way that it affects himself. This effect is the result of the author's interpretation of life, and the reader who effectively communicates the author's interpretation is reading interpretively.

At one time or another, all of us have heard literature read as if it were journalism—that is, the reader reading in an objective, reportorial manner. Although such a reader can be commended for being objective and unbiased in the face of life, he is not reading interpretively. He has disregarded the problem to be discussed in this chapter—what's the right interpretation?—by avoiding interpretation altogether. Perhaps he is not as unbiased as we thought.

Literature portrays a peculiar kind of life, a life that occasionally has little resemblance to real life, except in the basic truths of human nature. An author sifts life for details that will make his writing interesting. He edits life, he alters and changes, he fits life to his purpose. In short, he interprets life.

When the writing is good, our appreciation and enjoyment of life is increased, sometimes tremendously. At times we even share the feelings of Holden Caulfield, the hero of J. D. Salinger's *Catcher in the Rye:*

What really knocks me out is a book that, when you're all done reading it, you wish that the author that wrote it was a terrific friend of yours and you could call him up on the phone whenever you felt like it.

Since the reader re-creates the life first created by the author, he should re-create an experience that is justified by the writing—that is, in keeping with the author's interpretation. But even before the reader can consider whether or not he is making the right interpretation of the author's work, he must be certain of one all-important matter—namely, that he *has* an interpretation. To paraphrase Abe Lincoln's quip which recommended that it was better to remain silent and be thought dumb than to speak up and remove all doubt, it's better to excuse yourself and not read than to read lifelessly, without interpretation, and disappoint the audience altogether. Interpretation implies life, and the reader's first responsibility is to read with a feeling for life, if he can hope to make the writing live for his audience.

Again, during the first few readings, no one can expect to read "with a feeling for life" as well as he would like to. Experience teaches us how to express the feeling that we have. And as has been mentioned before, knowing that the audience would like to be entertained, and therefore wants you to do well, is the first step toward development of your ability to re-create the life in literature.

THE RIGHT INTERPRETATION

Having briefly examined the nature of interpretation, we arrive at the primary concern of this chapter: the right interpretation. To preface the matter of right versus wrong interpretations, it should be noted that several right and many wrong interpretations of a single work are possible. And with that prefatory remark to investigate, we'll proceed to find out whether or not such a statement is at all valid.

We'll begin with a simple sentence which I will write for you to read aloud: **This print is very black.** (You'll immediately recognize that the sample sentence is somewhat removed from the "feeling for life" mentioned earlier, but the example suits our present purpose, which is to base interpretation upon meaning.)

We'll assume that the simple sample sentence is taken from an essay. If we describe three different contexts for the sentence, there will be three different interpretive readings of the sentence:

1. The essay is written with a supreme disgust for heavy black print;
2. The essay is written about the development of many different types and colors of print, but is only concerned with *this* print at the moment;
3. The essay is written with a firm conviction that print should be black, heavy black, and never anything but heavy black.

The difficulty of the three interpretations is graded, the third being the most subtle to read effectively. But the main purpose of these three interpretations is to illustrate a point made in Chapter Three: the sound of the reading is determined by the meaning of the writing. In short, you read what you mean.

The above exercise served to illustrate the different interpretations possible for a single sentence when the context of the sentence is changed. Now turning to a passage which has a fixed meaning, we'll see how it is possible to have more than one "right" interpretation of a writing:

> Tomorrow, and tomorrow, and tomorrow
> Creeps in this petty pace from day to day,
> To the last syllable of recorded time;
> And all our yesterdays have lighted fools
> The way to dusty death. Out, out, brief candle!
> Life's but a walking shadow, a poor player
> That struts and frets his hour upon the stage,
> And then is heard no more; it is a tale
> Told by an idiot, full of sound and fury,
> Signifying nothing.

This soliloquy from Shakespeare's *Macbeth* has been interpreted in several different ways. Two of the most prevalent interpretations are these:

1. Macbeth is a strong, ambitious man, a poet-soldier who is becoming painfully aware of the futility of his vaulting ambition to be king. The soliloquy is read as if Macbeth were *embittered* by the pessimistic and cynical truth which his words uncover.
2. Macbeth, a sensitive man who is spurred on by the galloping ambition of his Lady, at last faces the truth of his circumstances. The soliloquy is read as if Macbeth were momentarily giving in to despair; he speaks almost *mournfully*.

It is possible to have two or more right interpretations of a single writing, so long as an interpretation is justified by the writing. A wrong interpretation of Macbeth's soliloquy would be a reading which has Macbeth take a Socratic delight in discovering a truth—wrong because Macbeth wasn't much of a thinker, and Macbeth having just received news of Lady Macbeth's death, the time isn't right for delight, however Socratic it may be.

Consider Hyman Kaplan's interpretation of Macbeth's soliloquy. Mr. Kaplan, the fictitious creation of Leonard Q. Ross, is enrolled in a night class for the foreign-born. He has been eagerly rebuffing the comments which his classmates have made on the soliloquy, and his teacher, Mr. Parkhill, sensing that Hyman Kaplan may really have something worthwhile to contribute, asks him to take his turn in the Recitation and Speech period:

Mr. Kaplan's face broke into a glow; his smile was like a rainbow. "Soitinly," he said, walking to the front of the room. Never had he seemed so dignified, so eager, so conscious of a great destiny.

"Er—Mr. Kaplan," added Mr. Parkhill, suddenly aware of the possibilities which the situation (Kaplan on Shakespeare) involved: "Speak *carefully*."

"*Spacially* careful vill I be," Mr. Kaplan reassured him. He cleared his throat, adjusted his tie, and began: "Ladies an' gantleman, you hoid all kinds minninks abot dis piece poyetry, an'—"

"*Poetry*."

"—abot dis piece *poetry*. But to me is a difference minnink altogadder. Ve mus' tink abot Julius Scissor an' how *he* falt!"

Mr. Parkhill moved nervously, puzzled.

"In dese exact voids is Julius Scissor sayink—"

"Er—Mr. Kaplan," said Mr. Parkhill once he grasped the full import of Mr. Kaplan's error. "The passage is from 'Macbeth'."

Mr. Kaplan looked at Mr. Parkhill with injured surprise. "*Not* from 'Julius Scissor'?" There was pain in his voice.

"No. And it's—er—'Julius C*ae*sar'."

Mr. Kaplan waited until the last echo of the name had permeated his soul. "Podden me, Mr. Pockheel. Isn't '*seezor*' vat you cotting somting op mit?"

"That," said Mr. Parkhill quickly, "is 'scissor.' You have used 'Caesar' for 'scissor' and 'scissor' for 'Caesar'."

Mr. Kaplan nodded, marvelling at his own virtuosity.

"But go on with your speech, please." Mr. Parkhill, to tell the truth, felt a little guilty that he had not announced at the very beginning that the passage was from "Macbeth." "Tell us *why* you thought the lines were from 'Julius Caesar'."

"Vell," said Mr. Kaplan to the class, his smile assuming its normal serenity. "I vas positiff, becawss I can *see* de whole ting." He paused, debating how to explain this cryptic remark. Then his eyes filled with a strange enchantment. "I see de whole scinn. It's in a tant, on de night bafore dey makink Julius de Kink fromm Rome. So he is axcited an' ken't slip. He is layink in bed, tinking: 'Tomorrow an' tomorrow an' tomorrow. How slow dey movink! Almost cripps! Soch a pity de pace!'"

Before Mr. Parkhill could explain that "petty pace" did not mean "Soch a pity de pace!" Mr. Kaplan had soared on.

"De day go slow, from day to day like lettle tsyllables on phonograph racords fromm time."

Anxiety and bewilderment invaded Mr. Parkhill's eyes.

"'An' vat about yestiddy?' tinks Julius Scissor. Ha! 'All our yestiddays are only makink a good light for fools to die in de dost!'"

"'Dusty death' doesn't mean—" There was no interrupting Mr. Kaplan.

"An' Julius Scissor is so tired, an' he vants to fallink aslip. So he hollers, mit fillink, 'Go ot! Go ot! Short Candle!' So it goes ot."

Mr. Kaplan's voice dropped to a whisper. "But he ken't slip. Now is bodderink de idea fromm life. 'Vat is de life altogadder?' tinks Julius Scissor. An' he gives ensver, de pot I like de bast. Life is like a bum actor, strottink an' hollerink around de stage for only vun hour bafore he's kicked ot. Life is a tale told by idjots, dat's all, full of fonny sonds an' phooey!"

Mr. Parkhill could be silent no longer. "'Full of sound and fury!'" he cried desperately. But inspiration, like an irresistible force, swept Mr. Kaplan on.

" 'Life is monkey business! It don' minn a ting. It signifies nottink!' An' den Julius Scissor closes his ice fest—" Mr. Kaplan demonstrated the Consul's exact ocular process in closing his "ice"—"an' falls dad!"

The class was hushed as Mr. Kaplan stopped. In the silence, a tribute to the fertility of Mr. Kaplan's imagination and the power of his oratory, Mr. Kaplan went to his seat. But just before he sat down, as if adding a postscript, he sighed: "Dat vas mine idea. But ufcawss is all wronk, becawss Mr. Pockheel said de voids ain't bot Julius Scissor altogadder. It's all abot an Irishman by de name Macbat."

Then Mr. Kaplan sat down.

It's obvious that Hyman Kaplan has taken a pretty literal road to Rome, and that his trip has not been hampered by any consideration for imagery, rhythm, or similar tourist attractions. Even so, it's hard to deny that Hyman Kaplan's strong feeling for life has made his misguided understanding of the passage almost as stimulating (if not, infinitely more humorous) than a more valid interpretation.

There is another facet to the validity of an interpretation. A bit earlier it was noted that an interpretation is right when it is supported by, or justified in, the writing. Since it is possible to have several different right interpretations of a selection, there must be another way of determining which interpretation is best and right for you. There *is* another way, and it may well prove to be your greatest aid in developing an interpretation: conviction in the author's point of view.

Since the nature of interpretation in theatre and reading aloud are basically the same, and since we have heard "sad stories of the death of kings" in Shakespeare's realm, we might turn to the example of a distinguished theatre director who enjoyed success with a production of *Henry IV*, Part 1. Mr. Jules Irving, a director of New York's Lincoln Center, saw a parallel between the personalities and goals of Prince Hal, who would later become King Henry V, and Senator Jack Kennedy, who would later become President John F. Kennedy. Mr. Irving's production was infused with an immediacy that captured the audience's attention. This is the essence of Irving's point of view:

Both Prince Hal and Jack Kennedy were destined for leadership, and each prepared himself diligently for the responsibilities of national high office. Although delighting in the escapades which he shared with Falstaff, Prince Hal was keenly aware that he would one day be King, and his youthful conspiracies with Falstaff were always measured against a responsible effort to prepare himself for the future. Likewise, Jack Kennedy was single-minded in his determination to prepare for the responsibilities of the Presidency, and his every move as a young politician was dedicated to further not only his career but his ability to cope with the nation's problems as well. Director Irving, who knew that Shakespeare had chronicled the formative years in the character of Prince Hal, interpreted the author's point of view, and related it to his own knowledge of the making of a President.

A firm conviction in the author's point of view—that is, *believing* in the interpretation which you have arrived at—is as essential to effective reading as is speech. If the interpretation, or understanding of what the author is doing, isn't developed during the practice sessions of the reading, a reader is almost certain to feel unsure of his reading.

You should be able to state your interpretation of the selection in a few words. With the interpretation in mind, you'll find that the meaning of the selection will come into a sharper focus:

1. Character relations become more understandable;
2. The reason for the setting, mood, or story being drawn in the way it is becomes meaningful;
3. In short, all the literary aspects of the selection fall more neatly into place and take on added significance for you.

Often, when you apply your interpretation to the selection, the results are eye-opening, almost as if you had walked into a dark room and turned on the light.

Let us look at a final example from the poetry of Shakespeare, who reveals Hamlet as he is momentarily obsessed with the treachery involving his mother:

> O villain, villain, smiling, damned villain!
> . . .
> That one may smile, and smile, and be a villain!

Referring to his mother, is Hamlet saying "*that* one" (his mother) may smile, and smile, and yet be a villain? Or is his reference more general: that any person may smile, and smile, and still be a villain?

Whichever way you go, you have an interpretation, and the enlightenment and assurance that comes with it. Selecting the right interpretation will depend upon the evidence you can find in the rest of the play to support your point of view.

Having a belief in what you're reading, a belief that you're interpreting the selection the right way, is one of the surest ways of getting the right kind of response from the audience.

THE RIGHT INTERPRETATION ON TIME

Whether you read in a class, or at a club meeting, or on the radio, there is a time limitation made necessary by the programming. More often than not, the selection chosen for reading must be cut, and in such a way that your interpretation is unimpaired by the cutting. Using your interpretation as a guide, you can afterwards check each part of the cutting to assure yourself of having a uniform and coherent selection to read.

The excerpt taken from *The Education of Hyman Kaplan* would take approximately six minutes to read aloud. If the reading time were set at five minutes, you would cut those parts that are less critical to your interpretation. A segment suggesting a part of the cutting appears below:

· Mr. Kaplan's ~~face broke into a glow; his~~ smile was like a (1) rainbow. "Soitinly," he said, walking to the front of the room. Never had he seemed so dignified, so eager, so conscious of a great destiny.

"Er—Mr. Kaplan," added Mr. Parkhill, ~~suddenly aware of the~~ (2) ~~possibilities which the situation (Kaplan on Shakespeare) involved.~~ "Speak *carefully*."

"*Spacially* careful vill I be," Mr. Kaplan ~~reassured him. He~~ (3) cleared his throat, adjusted his tie, and began: "Ladies an' Gantleman, you hoid all kinds minninks abot dis piece poyetry, an'—"

"*Po*etry."

"—abot dis piece *po*etry. But to me is a difference minnink altogadder. Ve mus' tink abot Julius Scissor an' how *he* falt!"

Mr. Parkhill moved nervously, puzzled.

"In dese exact voids is Julius Scissor sayink—"

"Er—Mr. Kaplan," ~~said Mr. Parkhill once he grasped the full~~ (4) ~~impact of Mr. Kaplan's error.~~ "The passage is from 'Macbeth'."

Mr. Kaplan looked at Mr. Parkhill with injured surprise.

"*Not* from 'Julius Scissor'?" ~~There was pain in his voice.~~ (5)

"No. And it's—er—'Julius C*ae*sar'."

To briefly explain the reasons for the above cutting—a cutting which could be more severe —we'll examine each of the cuts:

1. Although we lose the rhythm and rhyme of "glow" and "rainbow" in the opening sentence, there is a basic emotional reaction described in two different ways, and one of them can be cut. The paragraph's last sentence, seemingly ripe for cutting, sets up an excellent contrast for "tink abot Julius Scissor an' how *he* falt!" and therefore has been kept for its comic value.

2. The dialogue can be read to express Parkhill's "sudden awareness," making the (cut) explanation unnecessary. The "Er" is a characteristic sound of Parkhill's, and has been kept throughout because it will help the audience to identify Parkhill each time the sound is heard.

3. A typical time-limit compression. Since Kaplan's dialect is so distinctive and easily identified by the audience, most of the "Mr. Kaplan said" notations can be cut. Regarding Kaplan's dialect, a reader need only suggest the dialect and not attempt to give it a full, colorful expression.

4. Again, the dialogue can be read to express Parkhill's reaction—here, a sense of the need for immediate correction.

5. Kaplan's "pain" can be expressed in the reading of the dialogue. The first sentence of this brief paragraph may also be cut, but if it is cut, a pause will probably be needed to compensate for the loss. This first sentence not only tells us that Kaplan confronts "Macbeth" with "injured surprise," the sentence also gives the audience time to weigh the effect of the news on Kaplan, who till this time was "so dignified, so eager, so conscious of a great destiny."

Cutting the selection is a justifiable action, and most often a necessary one. In many selections you will find it necessary to cut whole paragraphs and speeches in order to stay within the time limit and keep your audience's attention focused on the most significant parts of the selection. When making extensive, deep cuttings in a selection, read the cutting carefully afterwards to see that the selection still has its normal flow of thought. The audience is perplexed by a skeletal cutting that disrupts their train of thought, just as any audience would be baffled to hear a speaker begin a talk with "However . . . ."

At times, it may be necessary to *add* as well as cut, usually when you see that a gap has resulted from the cutting. You add to a selection in order to make your reading clear, and there is one instance of the need for adding in the above cutting of *Hyman Kaplan*.

At one point Parkhill corrects Kaplan's pronunciation of "poyetry." You would be justified in rewriting the line to read as follows:

"*Po*etry," Mr. Parkhill corrected.

This rewriting serves to break up the staccato, which is so delightful to the eye but so confusing to the ear in this instance, and identifies the speaker as being Parkhill. A more dramatic way of rewriting this part would be to insert "Er—" in front of Parkhill's "*Po*etry."

Both rewritings are in the style of the author, an extremely important consideration in itself. Which rewriting do you choose? The first one, which is somewhat pedantic and yet in keeping with Parkhill's classroom situation? Or the second, more dramatic one? Which one is more in keeping with your interpretation?

By illustrating certain aspects of the right interpretation—namely, *having* an interpretation; testing its validity by examination of the author's point of view; and cutting a selection within the framework of an interpretation—three basic forms of literature have been introduced; prose, poetry, and drama. Since each of your selections falls into one of these three categories, each of the three forms will now be considered in greater detail.

Chapter Six

PROSE

Before too many students of literature become offended, it should be noted that prose is not a literary form. Prose is the common language, and as the common language, it embraces all literary forms. Paradoxically, the term "prose" is used most often with reference to basic types of writing: exposition, description, narration, and argument, none of which are literary forms.

That one writing is a certain form and that another writing is of a different form is one of your concerns as a reader. However, although classification has its value—especially to the writer, scholar, critic and teacher, who use their understanding of forms to enhance their work—for the reader, there is a more important consideration: how does the writing affect a reading? Each basic type of writing (exposition, description, narration and argument) affects the reading in a slightly different way.

Exposition

Expository prose "exposes," or lays open, the subject. This is writing that informs and explains—how something operates, a sequence of events, how to play bridge, a person's opinion—and as such, exposition has been called the workhorse of written communications. By the sheer number of people writing expository prose everyday in business, in government, in education, and in their homes, more creativity is channeled into exposition than any other basic type of writing.

Of course, the creativity doesn't end with the writing. Exposition makes its demands upon the reader's creativity, as well, for this type of writing isn't so much "factual prose" to be transmitted for the audience's consumption. For example, take the plight of Robinson Crusoe, the famous creation of Daniel Defoe. In the following paragraph, Defoe explains Robinson Crusoe's reasons for selecting a camp site on his castaway island:

I consulted several things in my situation, which I found would be proper for me: first, health and fresh water; secondly, shelter from the heat of the sun; thirdly, security from ravenous creatures, whether men or beasts; fourthly, a view to the sea, that if God sent any ship in sight, I might not lose any advantage for my deliverance, of which I was not willing to banish all my expectation yet.

The creative, or interpretive, reader will not only make clear each of Crusoe's four requirements for a suitable dwelling place but will also imply, in his reading, the urgency, the need, the desperate state of Robinson Crusoe and his hope for survival. The character's troubled state of mind is suggested by such words as "ravenous," "beasts," and "God," which give expository prose a vitality not normally associated with "factual prose."

To be brief in describing how the nature of exposition affects a reading, there is a reason behind every fact, and an attitude behind every statement. The creative reader will discover that reason or attitude, and color his reading with it, thereby giving the selection its total meaning. Although exposition may be somewhat objective in its "exposing" a subject, it deals most often with life, which is the realm of the reader, and therefore justifies emotions in the reader's vocal and physical expressions. Too much emotion may sound and look extravagant, and may even smother the facts, but nonetheless, for the reader, emotional expression will make the workhorse of written communications seem the thoroughbred he really is, powerful, lean and purposeful.

Description

Descriptive prose is concerned with details, and details come to us through our senses: sight, sound, taste, smell, and touch. The details in the world of nature, in the world of people, come to the senses of the author, and the reader is the middleman, the audience's bridge to an enriched appreciation of the author's observation of our world.

One of the world's most perceptive observers was Aldous Huxley, whose *Brave New World* was alarming not so much for its appeal to our senses, but for the sense it made. The opening paragraph of his essay "Music at Night" illustrates an author's sensory appeal in descriptive prose:

Moonless, this June night is all the more alive with stars. Its darkness is perfumed with faint gusts from the blossoming lime trees, with the smell of wetted earth and the invisible greenness of the vines. There is silence; but a silence that breathes with the soft breathing of the sea, and the thin shrill noise of a cricket, insistently, incessantly harps on the fact of its own deep perfection. Far away, the passage of a train is like a long caress, moving gently, with an inexorable gentleness, across the warm living body of the night.

Directly and indirectly, Huxley appeals to each of the senses, and the euphoric balm and images in the writing can make an audience in school or college look forward to June, notwithstanding the (balmy) final examinations which that month brings.

In descriptive prose, the sense impressions are emphasized by the reader. Since the mind is capable of responding to the author's sense impressions with super-computer swiftness, the reader doesn't have to read slowly in order to give the audience time to experience the description. However, the reader should take time to let the audience's imagination savor those descriptive details that are most important to the meaning of the selection. For example, the appeal to sound would be emphasized in the reading of the above paragraph from Huxley's "Music at Night," which later develops into an inquiry on the nature of music, and such words as "silence," "harps," and "passage" can be stressed to reinforce the author's concern for music.

Finally, descriptive prose in literature often suggests a mood—a mood of serenity or chaos, of glimmer or gloom, of buoyancy or depression—and as mentioned before, the mood of the selection should not only be reflected in the reading, but reflected *early* in the reading in order to get the audience involved with the selection at the outset.

Narration

Narration, or storytelling, is probably the reader's most popular type of writing, for nearly everyone enjoys hearing a story. A travelogue, a mountain-climbing adventure, a trip to the moon— whether it's fact or fiction, the audience is anxious to sojourn with the narrator.

In descriptive prose, when a man's appearance and manner are being described, the man's character is being revealed as well. Often a man's character will also be revealed in a narration, which relates his actions. And sometimes the three (description, characterization, and narration) are integrated within a single writing, as in the case of the excerpt appearing below.

In Audie Murphy's *To Hell and Back,* a sergeant is leading his platoon in an assault on an enemy position. He has been knocked to the ground by fire three times:

Fascinated, we watch as he gets up for the third time and dashes straight into the enemy fire. The Germans throw everything they have at him. He falls to the earth; and when he again pulls himself to his feet, we see that his right arm is shattered. But wedging his gun in his left arm-pit, he continues firing and staggers forward. Ten horrified Germans throw down their guns and yell, *"Kamerad."*

Although there are elements of striking description and characterization in this passage, the story of the sergeant's forward progression (the narration) is the major interest.

How does the nature of narration affect the reading? The rate and intensity of the reading will rise and fall with the high and low interest points of the story. However, since narration seldomly requires the audience to think over what they are hearing, the reader's rate for narration is often a bit faster than normal. Not appreciably faster, to be sure, but fast enough to keep the audience from getting ahead of the reader.

Regarding characterization that is found in most narrative selections, you will find that some authors assume a character as they write, and write in the first person, as in the case of Twain's *Huckleberry Finn* and Salinger's *Catcher in the Rye.* In order to give the selection its full meaning, the reader will suggest the character of the person who is narrating, and involved in, the action.

In addition to the narrator, other characters are involved in the story, and the natures of most of these characters are revealed in dialogue, or characters' speeches.

Dialogue has been treated briefly in the *Hyman Kaplan* selection of the preceding chapter, and will be treated at greater length in Chapter Eight.[1] It should be noted here that dialogue not only provides a relief from the descriptive and narrative parts of the selection, the dialogue often reveals thoughts and actions that the descriptive and narrative parts have been leading up to.

The narration which has no dialogue often builds in interest until it culminates in a climactic passage containing dialogue. Therefore, controlling your reading so that you build the audience's interest in the reading—in other words, building to the climaxes—is a matter of great importance, and the rhythms of the language, not to mention the nature of any character involved in the story, should be comfortably in your command by the time you've finished your preparation and practice sessions.

Argument

With regard to writing, an argument is not a fight or quarrel, the result of tempers flaring up. On the contrary, reason, proof, and evidence are the main combatants in an argument, not tempers, and logic is often the argument's most fiery asset.

The author has an opinion, and he writes to express his opinion persuasively. He hopes for acceptance of his argument, by merit of the evidence used to prove his point. If his writing also recommends a course of action to correct something which he feels is wrong, his writing is proof of the fact that argument, as a basic type of writing, is not a bloodless examination of truth and liberty, but a vital concern for injustice, false values, and inhumanity. In short, a concern for the crucial issues of life.

Consider this excerpt from *Notes of a Native Son* by James Baldwin:

---

[1] Chapter Eight describes methods that will help the audience to distinguish between the various characters in the reading.

At the root of the American Negro problem is the necessity of the American white man to find a way of living with the Negro in order to be able to live with himself. And the history of this problem can be reduced to the means used by Americans—lynch law and law, segregation and legal acceptance, terrorization and concession—either to come to terms with this necessity, or to find a way around it, or (most usually) to find a way of doing both these things at once. The resulting spectacle, at once foolish and dreadful, led someone to make the quite accurate observation that "the Negro-in-America is a form of insanity which overtakes white men."

Baldwin is concerned with a vital issue of modern society.

The argument is designed to prove a point, and makes its appeal to the audience's sense of reason and right. When an author is extremely persuasive in his argument, he will also make an appeal to the reader's emotions, in a further attempt to win the reader's support. Therefore, although the argument makes its appeal primarily to the intellect, the reader can communicate emotional connotations without fear of hindering the audience's mental stimulation.

The matter of mental stimulation suggests one pertinent consideration for the reader. An argument is food for thought, and the audience should be given ample time to assimilate the ideas and proofs which they're hearing. Generally, then, a slower rate of reading combined with pauses (longer and more frequent than normal) is preferred for argumentative prose. The reading may seem a bit heavy during your first practice sessions, but the method proves effective with the audience—especially when the author's main point is foremost in your mind, for then the argument is more likely to be foremost in the mind of the audience.

Whether you read Bertrand Russell writing against bombs and destruction, or John Stuart Mill writing on the value of liberty, or Vincent van Gogh writing on the morality of art, you are coming in touch with minds capable of expressing strong feelings in rational, convincing argumentative prose.

FICTION

For the reader's purpose, the distinction between fiction (short story, novel and novella) and non-fiction prose (biography, essay, document and journal) isn't profoundly significant. Both fiction and non-fiction prose employ exposition, description, narration, and argument to achieve their ends. Moreover, both fiction and non-fiction are based largely on the actions of man, and therefore the reader deals with material of human interest in both instances.

However, most audiences prefer hearing fiction to non-fiction, chiefly because fiction often has more continuity of action, or a story. Although it would be pointless (and downright wrong) to say that fiction is more artful than non-fiction, writers of fiction use a wide range of literary techniques and devices not always available to writers of non-fiction.

The Short Story and the Novel

It was William Faulkner who said, "Maybe every novelist wants to write poetry, finds he can't, and then tries the short story, which is the most demanding form after poetry. And, failing at that, only then does he take up novel writing." Faulkner implies, bypassing the poetry for the moment, that the short story is more challenging than the novel, or, at least, different from the novel.

With few exceptions, the short story is briefer than the novel. To compensate for its brevity, the short story is more compressed, and five hundred words of a short story accomplishes more than the same number of words in a novel. The short story is more intense and necessarily has greater unity.

This tense compression of life in the short story will be felt by the audience, even when you do not work to suggest the intensity in your reading. The expression of the short story's compression in a reading isn't essential always, and in some cases, it may even beat a short story to death, making heavy what was already very intense. Intensity in the reading is justified in many instances, however, especially when the short story is more introspective and has a story line that is not forcefully drawn.

More importantly, since the short story must accomplish more in fewer words than the novel, each word in a short story serves more than one literary function at a time. Consequently, there is an extensive use of symbolism in the short story, more association and interrelating of ideas and images, more frequent variations on the same theme.

This is where the nature of the short story has its greatest effect on the reading. The reader repeats a tone used earlier in the reading to suggest a similarity between ideas appearing at different points in the story; he lowers his volume when reading one passage to associate it with an earlier passage, which was also read in a low volume; he repeats a staccato rendering to relate one idea to another. In short, the reader echoes and reinforces the association of words and ideas appearing in the short story.

Although the novel is less compressed than the short story, the reader cannot sprawl, relaxed and at ease, for the novel is not all that less intense. While the short story delineates one idea in a relatively short space, the novel covers a great deal more—sometimes whole histories of families—and often moves at a hell-for-leather pace. No, the reader practices all the facets of his craft when reading from a novel, and if anything is exceptional in reading an excerpt from a novel, it is likely to be the climaxes. The reader is especially mindful of building to the climaxes, building and relaxing the audience's interest in the writing, particularly for the longer readings.

The refined reading approach described for the short story is not easy, and the more complex the literary form, the more challenging is the reading. Of course, the ultimate in this refined approach is the reading of poetry, with its wordplay and connotations, repetition of rhythms and sounds, and close association of images and moods.

The reading of poetry, which is *the* most compressed literary form, is discussed in the chapter that follows.

Chapter Seven

POETRY

Poetry is audience literature. It is meant to be read aloud to people, and even when read in private, poetry means more when it is heard, for the sound of the poem uncovers meanings that escape the eye.

When reading prose silently the eye often scans the writing, and although there may be words and expressions which escape our attention, we nevertheless get a fairly good understanding of what the writing is about. If we silently breeze through the poetry selection, however, our understanding of the writing is considerably less than it might have been.

SOUND AND MOVEMENT

Silently read the celebrated first lines of Robert Browning's "How They Brought the Good News from Ghent to Aix":

> I sprang to the stirrup, and Joris, and he;
> I galloped, Dirck galloped, we galloped all three;

When reading the lines silently a glance tells us that there is some action here: a few men are in a hurry to get someplace. This is actually all the information we need to get from these two lines —and information is all that we *will* get from them when reading silently.

When the lines are read aloud, with even the slightest effort, we feel the motion of the writing. There is movement in the lines, and the sound of the writing stirs us physically. The reading aloud of the words gives us more than just information. It creates a physical activity which, however slight, is similar to the physical activity experienced by the horsemen in the poem. The reader and listener are physically involved with the action of the poem, and are likely to be more emotionally involved as a result.

The urgency of the news which the men are rushing to Aix is heard in the next two lines of the poem:

> "Good speed!" cried the watch, as the gatebolts undrew;
> "Speed!" echoed the wall to us galloping through;

The sound of "Good speed!", which is terse, intense, and a little frenetic, propels the horsemen on their mission. Their sense of purpose is sharpened by the watchman's cry, and the desperate echo of "Speed!" increases their anxiety as they thunder past the security of the city walls. The reader picks up the urgency of the horsemen's mission from the sound of their departure.

Now combining all six lines of the first stanza of the poem, the reader, with his sense of the acceleration in the above four lines, is better prepared to interpret the final two lines, which suggest that something may befall the ride of the horsemen:

> I sprang to the stirrup, and Joris, and he;
> I galloped, Dirck galloped, we galloped all three;
> "Good speed!" cried the watch, as the gatebolts undrew;
> "Speed!" echoed the wall to us galloping through;
> Behind shut the postern, the lights sank to rest,
> And into the midnight we galloped abreast.

Browning has deliberately slowed down the pace of the last two lines. The excitement of the men's departure is perhaps still felt within the city, but the horsemen have settled down into their ride and are moving forward into the night. Notice that Browning uses "midnight" and not "night" in the final line. He uses a word which not only gives him the rhythm he wants, but which also suggests the calm and suspense first felt by the horsemen as the poem opens into the night.

Obviously, this is not a definitive study of the excerpt from Browning's poem, and an inquiring student will discover many details that will lend strength to his own interpretation. The purpose of this brief examination has been to introduce a concern for sound and movement in the reading of poetry.

Although different types of poetry require different types of reading, the reader is consistently responsive to the tides and floods of the poem's language, for poetry is always in motion. Moreover, the sound of the poem is one of the reader's best guides to the poem's meaning.

READING DIFFERENT TYPES OF POETRY

It is pecisely this last statement—that the sound of the poem is a primary concern of the reader—which has caused so much debate regarding the reading of poetry. Contemporary poets, professional readers, and instructors keep the debate alive:

POET

My work is music, and whoever reads it like prose—pouncing on a single meaning and driving it home with all the versatility of a jack-hammer—that person has a tin ear and had better leave my work alone.

READER

I'll have to agree that your art is subtle and deserving of varied, refined techniques, but everything you people write isn't musical. And if your wrote more for the ear and less for the eye, I wouldn't have any problems in creating the textures you say you would like to hear. By the way, you apparently know nothing about the reading of prose.

INSTRUCTOR

One of you decries the lack of music in reading poetry, and the other retorts that poetry isn't always musical. I think that since you're both right, the Debate will go on forever. Incidentally, Reader, I've heard you read prose selections, and there are a few things I'd like to go over with you. . . .

While there are many schools of thought about the reading of poetry, most of them are in accord on the initial step of the reader: he eases into the poem. That is, the reader should let the poem do its own work by reading the poem silently a number of times before giving it full voice. Whether the poem should then be whispered several times, in order to dam up the poem's meanings even more before releasing them aloud, is another matter of debate, and will be determined only by your style and inclination. The rest of the matter—the reading itself—can be made more meaningful by an examination of the reading of various types of poetry.

Lyric

The lyric is an expression of feeling. It was given its name in ancient times, when the reader was accompanied by a lyre, and its origin is reflected in the nature of today's lyrics. The lyric is the most musical form of poetry.

Being the most musical, the lyric is the form which makes our Poet most critical about readers. He objects to the lyric being read as if it were living-room prose, understandably. He could object to its being chanted, although some readers render a lyric quite well with a chant-like expression that reveals the rhythms and colors of the language.

He seems to favor giving full expression to the natural music of the language, an approach that has proved most rewarding for the beginning reader. The approach emphasizes the poem's texture, or sensuous qualities of the poem's sounds, and that texture is never coarse.

Since the lyric is musical, does the reader sing? Literally, no— lyrically, yes. That is, the reader will be reading with music in his ears even though he isn't singing. The sound of such a reading can be imagined if you bring to mind a song being sung. First, take away the musical accompaniment; then take away the tune. What remains is a voice giving words their own melodious sounds, and the effect, when the lyric is rendered without affectation, is pleasant to the ears and stirring in its simplicity.

The simplicity of the lyric should occupy the reader's attention throughout the practice sessions. While the putting together of sounds in a meaningful way is anything but simple, the reader works to attain simplicity of emotional expression. One of the most satisfactory ways of attaining this simplicity is to avoid any rendering that is dramatic or theatrical. When the reading becomes dramatic, it's evident that the reader is trying too hard to make a point with an emotion. And an emotion does not make a point or comment in the lyric—the emotion simply is.

Another matter relating to the avoidance of dramatic reading is characterization. Neither the character of the poet nor the personality of the reader should come through appreciably in the reading. The lyric is an expression of feeling, which is a human quality, not the quality of a human.

This feeling is expressed by the sound of words and their meanings. Therefore, by way of emphasizing the significance of the music of the language, the reader will benefit from not trying to listen to himself. That is, he should hear the natural music of the words, not the music of his voice. A fine distinction, but an important one, for the lyrical simplicity of pure feeling can be easily lost when the reader doesn't surrender himself to the natural music of language.

Sonnet

The rhythm of a lyric may be sweeping, lightly rising and falling with each nuance of feeling. The rhythm is the flow of the language, and it does not always end with the end of the reading, for it may linger in the audience's memory for some time after the reading has ended.

The rhythm of the sonnet is similar to the rhythm of the lyric in that there is movement in each. The sonnet, however, is usually read with more precise regularity in rhythm, for good reason: the sonnet, as a form, is a tighter composition than other forms of poetry.

The sonnet is somewhat paragraphical, in that its parts are more clearly marked. Every sonnet has fourteen lines, no more or less. The Italian sonnet is "divided" into two parts, of eight lines and six lines. The English sonnet is comprised of three four-line units and a closing couplet. Each type of sonnet has a time-honored rhyme scheme, which rarely varies. The sonnet's form is well defined and orderly.

Orderly but not cold. Orderly but not broken up into separate compartments of emotions. The poet's emotions are as much a part of the sonnet as they are of the lyric, and they do not begin and end with each unit of the sonnet but rather they shift and change in the course of the sonnet. Although the poet may present a situation in the early part of the poem and a resolution in the last part of the poem, there is a continuity of attitude bridging the parts of the poem.

The English sonnet, however, often makes a marked shift of emotion and thought in the last two lines, almost as if everything in the poem has been building to the concluding couplet. The last two lines are usually epigrammatic, a summing up and an implication of truth. The Italian sonnet's concluding lines are not so severely conclusive as the English sonnet's, but still its last lines are a culmination of the poem's movement.

Therefore, the reader builds to the psychology and thought of the sonnet's last lines. And although he is obedient to the sense of time and rhyme of the language, he is also mindful of the lyrical quality of the sonnet and reflects the music of the language in his reading.

Narrative

Casey at the bat in Mudville and Achilles in a fury on the Trojan plain are characters in stories. Their stories are told in verse, Casey's being called a narrative and Achilles' being called an epic. The difference between the two (narrative and epic) lies in the nature of the poet's language, the epic being more majestic.

The progression and unfolding of the story is the reader's main concern. Of course, he is always mindful of the language of poetry, but the story must be told. Since so many narrative poems are written in evenly measured lines having prominent end-rhymes, particular attention should be paid to the rhythm of speech if the reader can expect to make the story meaningful.

You are familiar with the term sing-song. Taken separately, the words "sing" and "song" are appropriate to the reading of poetry. Combined, they are deadly. A reader wants to avoid the sing-song, almost as much as his audience wants to avoid hearing it.

The sing-song is the result of an overwhelming regard for a constant and unrelenting rhythm in verse that is evenly measured. Fortunately, there is a variety of means to conquer the sing-song effect:

Duration, the length of a time a sound is held, provides variation in the reading. Some sounds can be held, and should be held, longer than others.

Phrasing, the natural linking together of words in speech, is invaluable in reducing the sing-song effect and helps to enhance the communication of the story.

Pausing at various moments between the phrasing of the words helps to give the verse a more natural lilt.

And finally, there is the psychological, rather than the vocal, stressing of the rhymes. Only too often the end-rhymes are read with a mallet, giving the impression that end-rhymes are pegs to be hammered at regular intervals. The subtle and well-controlled coloring of the words that rhyme produces a much more agreeable effect, and more importantly, gives the poem the natural rhythmic balance which the poet intended it to have.

Satiric, Dramatic, and Free

The humor in many satiric and comic verses largely resides in the words that rhyme, and a swelling or psychological stressing of the rhymes will point up the humor. Generally, light comic verse is best read in a spirited mood, and the more biting satiric verses are often rendered well with a more austere tone.

The main difference between reading dramatic poetry and dramatic prose or drama lies in the coloring of the language. In both dramatic poetry and drama the characters are suggested in the reading, but in reading dramatic poetry more attention is given to what the character is saying. That is, the audience should be as impressed with the character's language as they are with the character himself.

Although free verse is written without a rhythmic metric pattern and usually without rhyme, the reading of free verse should sound as natural as any verse. This *vers libre* should not be confused with blank verse, which has a rhythmic pattern that is very close to the natural rhythm of speech. Free verse is written in line units and phrase units, and each unit is read with its own particular rhythm, it not being possible (or prudent) to superimpose an overall rhythm.

Ballad

The ballad is one of the simplest forms of poetry—deceptively simple. The reader should be aware that the ballad tells a story, usually a dramatic one, lyrically. Story, drama, and lyric—a more awesome combination would be hard to find. A hefty, dramatic rendering overwhelms the sensitive lyrical quality, and a great concern for lyricism can detract from the communication of the story.

The best balance would lie in this direction: keep the story foremost (as in narrative poetry) while giving the rhythm a light dramatic pulsation and the language its natural lyrical quality. A person who is a good story-teller is likely to read a ballad well if he gives enough attention to the poem's lyrical quality.

THE AUDIENCE IN THE MIDDLE

In this chapter on poetry, few references have been made to the audience. The explanation for this lies in the nature of poetry reading: poetry reading is more inner-directed than any other type of reading. The reader doesn't reach out to the audience as much as he does in reading a prose selection.

One authority even suggests that the reader should read a poem as if the audience could only hear and not see him. Another advocates that all poetry is essentially dramatic. This particular reader closes his eyes while reading poetry, and seems enraptured by what the poem gives him. He, in turn, gives the poem little, although it must be admitted that his visage is admirably dramatic.

One school of readers believes that the texture, or sensuous qualities of the language, must be given full play, emphasizing the poem's sound. Another school of readers advocates that the texture should be subdued by a rhythmic chanting which punctuates the rhymes and natural color of the language, emphasizing the poem's shape or form. Still another school, certainly the least credible of the three, finds that poetry is really prose after all and should be conversational in tone, emphasizing the art of conversation, perhaps.

In each of these schools, of course, there can be found the reader who emphasizes himself. This type of reader uses the poem as an excuse for "reading," and it seems a pity to him that the poem is there at all, he does so well by himself.

To comment on each of these schools of reading, it should be noted that each school has its values:

1. First of all, the texture of a poem is extremely important, though not all-important in the reading of all poems;
2. For the second school, the form and rhythmic balance of a poem convey much of the poem's meaning, though the musical sound of many poems equally conveys the meaning;
3. For the third school, a natural tone in the voice is desired over a forced, artificial tone, though naturalness should not be mistaken for a "conversational" or prosaic tone.

Depending upon the type of poem being read, types ranging from the lyric to the ballad, each of these approaches to poetry reading has its value.

There is one consideration that can help you to overcome the differences of opinion on poetry reading—the audience. In the reading of most poems the audience is in the middle, in between the reader and the poem, and an awareness of your relation to the audience can put to rest a number of vexing problems you might otherwise encounter in reading.

The normal sequence during a reading is author-reader-audience. That is, the author speaks to the audience through the reader, and the reader reaches out to the audience in order to communicate his selection. The reading of poetry, however, is more inner-directed, especially in the reading of lyrical poems, and solicits the audience's participation rather than extending out for it. The reader, then, is reading partly to himself and partly to the audience. At times, he will look directly to his audience and at other times withdraw, taking his audience's attention with him.

In the reading of poetry, there is more activity than the resonance of musical sounds, the balance of vowel and consonant, or
the play on words. There is an interplay of people—the meeting of
minds and the mutual generation of emotions between the reader
and the audience—and this communication between the reader
and his audience makes poetry reading one of the most spiritually
refreshing forms of reading aloud.

Since the poem is so unique in terms of structure and technique,
acute analysis of the intricate facets of the poem will result in an
invaluable understanding of the poem in performance. However, as
Dylan Thomas indicates in his "Poetic Manifesto," no reader can
afford to slight the subtle appeal of poetry, the subtleties not always
detectable in the most assiduous analysis:

You can tear a poem apart to see what makes it technically tick,
and say to yourself, when the words are laid out before you, the
vowels, the consonants, the rhymes and rhythms, "Yes, this is *it*.
This is why the poem moves me so. It is because of the craftsmanship". . . . The best craftsmanship always leaves holes and gaps in
the works of a poem so that something that is *not* in the poem can
creep, crawl, flash, or thunder in.

This something "not" in the poem comes from the reader who has
the will to find it in himself and communicate it.

Chapter Eight

DRAMA

Over three centuries ago Molière penned a comic character who, during a scene with his tutor, was amazed to discover that he had been speaking prose all his life and didn't know it. To inform him that he had also been speaking dialogue might have provided too much discovery for one sitting.

Dialogue—literally, an exchange of conversation—is the dramatist's medium, and it is written to be read aloud. Since, as the saying goes, a play is not written but rewritten, it comes to you audience-tested, and as such, drama is the only literary form that has been wrought (by a play*wright*) in the forge of audience response. When you select a scene that has a limited number of characters, you are assured of readable material.

Although there are passages of exposition, description, narration, and argument in a drama, they are spoken by characters, and are so much a part of the characters' thoughts, we're not impressed with the passages as being expository, descriptive, narrative, or argumentative. We're impressed with the characters and the action involving them.

READING THE PLAY

As mentioned in the first chapter, the reader does not act the play. The actor embodies part of a presentation or representation of life on the stage; the reader suggests that life. It is a matter of degree.

In a sense, reading a play is like reading fiction that has a great deal of dialogue. However, unlike the author of fiction, the playwright works almost exclusively through the dialogue of his characters. Occasionally a stage direction or character description will appear in the playscript, but primarily the characters tell the story. Therefore, when reading a play, the reader has greater liberty—you might say, greater need—to impersonate the characters. That is, he suggests the characters to a greater degree than he normally would while reading poetry or fiction.

It's apparent that your greatest work in preparation is with the characters: understanding the characters (their roles in the story and individual relationships with each other) and practicing the dialogue in order to assimilate the sound and meaning of the characters' speeches. Although there are plays with such a strong story-line that the characters seem secondary to the action, the reader still concentrates his work on the dialogue with an understanding that if there were no characters there would be no action.

When you have the selection prepared fairly well, you'll become aware of the challenge of reading from a play. The major challenge lies not so much in effectively reading the dialogue, but in distinguishing between the various characters, keeping them distinct and separate for the audience.

Distinguishing Between Characters

Two methods that help the audience to distinguish between the characters are (1) the consistent use of characterizations developed by the reader and (2) the placement of characters.

Regarding the consistency of each character you suggest in your reading, the same general traits of each character should be repeated each time a character appears in the reading. Although the character's rhythm and rate of speech, the look in his eyes, the sound of his voice and similar considerations may vary slightly from speech to speech—and sometimes from word to word—the character's traits will not change in any basic way, and should be suggested by the reader each time the character appears.

There are some basic traits of the character that do not change at all: his age, intelligence, emotional stability, and outlook on life. Conceivably, a character's emotional stability and outlook on life might change in the course of the play, but it is unlikely that any radical change in his nature will occur within the scene that you might choose to read. Therefore, the basic traits appropriate to each character are reflected with each character's appearance in the reading.

Regarding the second method of helping the audience to distinguish between characters—the placement of characters—often the audience can associate a character with a direction in which his particular speeches are read. You turn your shoulders a bit to the right, and read to the right, for one character; you read straight center for a second character; and read a bit to the left of center for a third character. This method is often employed in reading dialogue found in a work of fiction.

Something a bit more dramatic is needed for drama. A somewhat extreme method, extreme in the degree of character impersonation that the method usually requires, is one which has the reader turn his head abruptly toward center at the end of each character's speech. This signals to the audience that a different character is about to speak, and the audience will listen attentively in order to identify the character when the reader speaks. For scenes having speeches of considerable length and few characters, this method is very effective, for once the audience sees the abrupt head movement the reader can address any part of the audience during the character's speech.

The above method becomes difficult when there is a rapid exchange of dialogue, however, and the abruptness of the reader's head and shoulder movements can have a detrimental effect on the meaning of many plays. Therefore, a balance between the two methods—the straight-line direction (right, center, and left) and the abrupt turning of the head—is recommended.

Using the straight-line direction as a basis, you read all short speeches in predetermined directions. During the longer speeches, once the character has been identified by the direction in which you're reading, you read to all parts of the audience. Although it isn't essential that you return your gaze to the manuscript intermittently, a brief look at the manuscript can be used to indicate the end of one character's speech and, with a turn to a different set position, the beginning of another.

Since you aren't acting a play, but participating in it with your audience, you will have a great deal of eye contact—even when it's clear that the character speaking is supposedly unaware that an audience is watching him, as in the case of most modern dramas. Of course, as in poetry, your eye contact may be restrained at times and made impersonal when reading something of a very intimate nature, but still, the eye contact will give the audience the impression that you are participating in their discovery of the drama.

CUTTING DRAMA FOR READING

When cutting any selection, your work is guided not only by an interpretation but also by a consideration for the nature of the selection. The nature of drama does not permit much cutting, understandably, since the play has been written and rewritten to get a desired response from the audience.

The writing has been distilled. And since most dramas are based on those violent and sometimes questionable issues that arise from man's moral dilemmas, it is fire and not water that is distilled. For this reason, few literary forms are more capable of gripping the audience's intellect and emotions than drama.

To illustrate an extremely slight (but typical) cutting of a drama, a scene from Arthur Miller's *After The Fall* appears below. As a preface to the selection—and as a final reminder that a reader needn't employ theatre equipment to read drama effectively—a seemingly catastrophic incident regarding the touring version of the play will be described.

In 1965 the touring company performing *After The Fall* arrived in San Francisco for a two-week engagement. Since the play's premiere in New York, many critics had commented that the play revealed a close resemblance to Arthur Miller's marriage with Marilyn Monroe, and therefore San Francisco eagerly awaited the play that Miller had been working on for more than seven years. On opening night it was discovered that one of the vans carrying the theatre equipment had met with a highway accident. The opening performance was held with only part of the scenery and none of the light and sound equipment designed for the production.

Did the play stand on its own feet, with little support from its stage effects? A San Francisco drama critic wrote that *After The Fall* was "a tremendously rich and engrossing experience—one that drained me to the marrow." The critic's response to the play has an implication for the reader: no lack of stage effects can destroy the effectiveness of your reading, if you select a play of high quality and read it with skill. Should a reader select an insipid, sophomoric play, he will need all the help that he can get.

In the following excerpt, few lines have been cut and those only from stage directions. You'll notice that many key words and phrases are found at the ends of the lines, particularly in the more humorous speeches where the audience's laughter might otherwise cover a part of the speech.

The mood of the excerpt changes frequently—from light to serious, from serious to comic, and back to serious—and is evidence that drama is fortified by the shifting thoughts and feelings of its characters:

MAGGIE

Like to see my new apartment? There's no elevator even, or a doorman. Nobody would know. If you want to rest before you go to Washington. (He doesn't reply.) 'Cause I just found out—I go to Paris after London.

QUENTIN

So . . . how long will you be gone?

MAGGIE

It's maybe two months, I think. (They both arrive at the same awareness—the separation is pain. Tears are in her eyes.) Quentin?

QUENTIN

Honey . . . (Takes her hand) Don't look for anything more from me.

MAGGIE

I'm not! But if I went to Washington . . . I could register in the hotel as Miss None.

QUENTIN

N-u-n?

MAGGIE

No—"n-o-n-e"—like nothing. I made it up once 'cause I can never remember a fake name, so I just have to think of nothing and that's me! ~~(She laughs with joy.)~~ I've done it!

QUENTIN

It *is* a marvelous thought. The whole government's hating me, and meanwhile back at the hotel . . .

MAGGIE

That's what I mean! Just when that committee is knocking on your head you could think of me like naked—

QUENTIN

What a lovely thought!

MAGGIE

And it would make you happy.

QUENTIN

(Smiling warmly at her.) And nervous.

MAGGIE

Because it should all be one thing, you know? Helping people, and sex. You might even argue better the next day.

QUENTIN

~~(With a new awareness, astonishment)~~ You know? There's one word written on your forehead.

MAGGIE

What?

QUENTIN

"Now."

MAGGIE

But what else is there?

QUENTIN

A future. And I've been carrying it around all my life, like a vase that must never be dropped. So you can't ever touch anybody, you see?

In reading this scene, you would not read "Quentin" and "Maggie" aloud to identify the characters, for the audience can identify them when you employ the methods described earlier in the chapter. There may be times when you will want to read a character's name into certain stage directions. For example, taking a hypothetical dramatic situation, you might change "She picks up the revolver" to read "Gloria picks up the revolver," if the change were to make the reading clearer and more meaningful.

Not all scenes are suitable for reading aloud. In *After The Fall,* for example, there are many scenes that have crowds of people, some of them entering and exiting as if they were fantasies of Quentin's mind. The scenes most suitable for reading aloud are those that have few characters (preferably, not more than four), are climactic or comic, and are from the pens of master playwrights.

The final test for selecting a scene for reading is your response to it. If you respond to it well, chances are good that the drama will be well staged in the audience's imagination.

Chapter Nine

SOME PRACTICAL CONSIDERATIONS

Your instructor is your best guide to effective reading aloud. He reflects the audience's reaction to the reading, and his experience with literature and readers gives you direction in your development of the theory and technique of reading aloud. Not to be discounted by any means are the comments of your classmates, who have an acute awareness of the reading experience.

Still, there are a few considerations that warrant special mention here—considerations of a practical nature.

APPEARANCE OF THE READER

A part of the reader's appearance is his attire. Dress simply, but dress up. Most readers do dress appropriately. In fact, the proper appearance of most beginning readers prompted one instructor to say, "If some readers selected their reading materials as carefully as they selected the clothes they intended to wear for the readings, the effectiveness of their work might improve thirty to forty percent."

Strictly speaking, however, this section is concerned with the pre- and post-reading movements of the reader who sits in front of the audience, with particular interest in movements which appear to the audience even though the reader may not be fully aware of it.

If you arrive on the reader's platform or stage with the audience in view, be sure that you are instructed as to where you should sit. The game of musical chairs may be enjoyable at home, but can be embarrassing when played impromptu in view of an audience.

While sitting, avoid any overt gestures or movements that might detract from the attention being given the person in charge of the program. Take the chairman's introduction gracefully. It may be flattering, it may be (unintentionally) deflating. Relax by looking at the people who are listening to his introduction, and unless you are to enter into the reading as soon as you arrive at the reader's stand, thank the chairman for his comments.

When you arise from your chair, rise with your weight on the foot farthest from the reader's stand and make your first step with the foot nearest the reader's stand. A trifling consideration, but this writer has seen many readers heave themselves from their seats and wander about en route to the stand. It's apparent that such readers scarcely give their appearance any thought—much to the audience's displeasure, for a confident appearance in the reader's sitting, rising, and walking gives the audience an assurance that the reader knows what he is about.

When the reading is finished, remain at the stand long enough to gather your materials and let your audience know that the reading is over, then return directly to your chair. If the program permits applause, acknowledge the applause with a moderate nod while standing in front of your chair. You should feel the chair with the backs of your legs in order to sit without turning around to find the chair. If the applause is prolonged and appreciative, rise and acknowledge the applause again, this time nodding your appreciation to the chairman before resuming your seat.

KEEPING YOUR PLACE

Another practical consideration is the matter of keeping your place in the selection while you are reading. Without doubt, the best way to keep your place in the writing is to know the writing. You get to know the writing by practicing it aloud. There is no short cut.

Since we often learn a writing by associating memorable words and phrases with their placement on the printed page, it's been recommended that the beginning word or phrase of each paragraph appear in red when the writing is copied on a typewriter. The words in red help you to identify your place in the writing at a glance.

One method used infrequently is the thumb index. The thumb slides slowly down the edge of the page as you read, in time with your reading. This is unscientific at best, for most thumbs have minds of their own, but the method may be suited for you when reading from a stand.

The title of this section has another meaning—not only keeping your place in the writing, but keeping your place as a reader, as well. If you should lose your place while reading, the audience will not know unless you signal them in some way. Keep your poise, and if you need to scan your material in order to find your place, do so with quiet determination.

The time it takes to find your place is imperceptible. It may seem ages to you, but the audience will not notice it at all if they are not made aware of your plight. If a reader shrieks, "I'm lost!", in truth he's lost only after he has said it. The time taken to find your place (quietly, calmly) is well worth the investment. And of course, an even greater investment is the time spent in preparation, enabling you to be so familiar with the selection that you feel no anxiety about losing your place.

THE HANDS IN READING

The use of the hands in reading aloud has been described in earlier chapters. The matter is being considered now with reference to reading without a reader's stand, while the book or manuscript is held in the hands.

When the material reflects a hardened sentiment or violent action, the hand supporting the manuscript might be made into a fist. For more eloquent, majestic writing, the manuscript might rest on the back of the hand, palm out to the audience. (This last method can appear pretentious unless the writing is extremely powerful.) The fingers might be spread out into a fan for more relaxing, reflective writing, and held tightly together for more intense selections.

The implication of these remarks is that the audience observes your hands. The audience notices your hands, of course, for your eyes lead them in that direction at times. The point is that the hands are in a position to express a part of your reading, and while they may be inactive frequently, their appearance can be designed to reinforce the meaning of the writing.

Two fairly common practices of ill-practiced readers are worth mentioning: (1) Both hands gripping both sides of the manuscript and (2) hands that hold the manuscript too high. The first practice isn't functional when it comes time to turn a page, for neither hand is positioned to hold the manuscript by itself. The second practice forces the reader to look out narrowly over the top of the page, and may even block some of the audience's view of the reader's face. Regarding the matter of the manuscript's height, however, the materials shouldn't be held too low, for the throat can become constricted if the reader has to look down to a low level.

THE INTRODUCTION

The practicality of an introduction is evident. The information provided by the reader's introduction can make a reading more meaningful for the audience, and that is justification in itself.

However, there may be occasions when time does not permit much of an introduction beyond the mention of the selection's title and the name of the author. When the introduction has been reduced to title and author, read the first part of the selection a bit more slowly than normal, especially when you are following another reader. To compensate for the absence of an introduction that would prepare the audience for what they're about to hear, you will be giving the audience time to adjust to you and the author's work.

When time permits an introduction to the reading, take full advantage of it:

1. Reflect the tone (serious or light) of the selection with your introductory remarks;
2. Describe your reason for choosing the selection (historical, sociological, philosophical, or literary significance of the selection);

3. Relate the selection to something which is familiar to every member of the audience;
4. Describe the way in which the author's background or philosophy is pertinent to the selection, when applicable;
5. When reading an excerpt from a selection, supply sufficient background information on the entire selection.

The basic ingredients of the introduction will vary from reading to reading, but the primary purpose of the introduction remains the same: to make the reading more meaningful to the audience. The introduction itself will be more meaningful when it is delivered with spontaneity and not read from a manuscript.

One final thought: don't give the audience an abundance of information in the introduction. There is a possibility of explaining too much, and allowing the audience's imagination to go unchallenged. The first words of the reading should put the audience to work, and if the introduction has stirred interest in the selection, the audience is more likely to work with increasing pleasure to the end.

I think it is fitting to close this chapter, and the major part of this book, with comments on the introduction. The juxtaposition of conclusion and introduction suggests the close relationship of the author, the reader, and the audience: where the work of one ends, the work of another begins.

Your best work as a reader—it becomes less of a task and more of a pleasure as you develop your reading abilities—is beginning as you end this brief introduction to reading aloud.

Chapter Ten

SUGGESTED READINGS AND ASSIGNMENTS

This chapter is divided into two parts: (1) a list of authors whose works are suitable for (2) the suggested assignments. Regarding the list of recommended authors, although no author is named more than once, many of the authors have achieved fame in two or more literary forms.

RECOMMENDED AUTHORS

A American	*F* French	*I* Irish	*R* Russian
B Belgian	*G* German	*It* Italian	*S* Spanish
C Canadian	*Gr* Greek	*N* Norwegian	*Sc* Scottish
E English	*H* Hungarian	*P* Persian	*Sw* Swedish
		Po Polish	*W* Welsh

PROSE

Autobiography and Biography

Boswell, James (*E* 1740–95)
Bowen, Catherine (*A* 1897–)
Carnegie, Dale (*A* 1888–)
Chaplin, Charlie (*A* 1889–)
Clark, Barrett H. (*A* 1890–1953)
De Kruif, Paul (*A* 1890–)
Eastman, Max (*A* 1883–)
Franklin, Benjamin (*A* 1706–90)
Hart, Moss (*A* 1904–61)

Ludwig, Emil (*G* 1881–1948)
Maurois, Andre, (*F* 1885–)
Pearson, Hesketh (*E* 1887–1964)
Rogers, Will (*A* 1879–1935)
Sinclair, Upton (*A* 1878–)
Strachey, G. Lytton (*E* 1880–1932)
Thomas, Lowell (*A* 1892–)

Essays (Formal and Informal)

Addison, Joseph (*E* 1672–1719)
Bacon, Francis (*E* 1561–1626)

Baldwin, James (*A* 1924–)
Benchley, Robert (*A* 1889–1945)

Bergson, Henri (*F* 1859–1941)
Buchwald, Art (*A* 1925–)
De Quincey, Thomas (*E* 1785–1859)
Eiseley, Loren (*A* 1907–)
Emerson, Ralph W. (*A* 1803–82)
Golden, Harry (*A* 1902–)
Huxley, Aldous (*A* 1894–1964)
Johnson, Samuel (*E* 1696–1772)

Lamb, Charles (*E* 1775–1834)
Mencken, H. L. (*A* 1880–1956)
Mill, John Stuart (*E* 1806–73)
Perelman, S. J. (*E* 1904–)
Pyle, Ernie, (*A* 1900–1945)
Russell, Bertrand (*E* 1872–)
White, E. B. (*A* 1899–)
Woolf, Virginia (*E* 1882–1941)

Miscellany

Carson, Rachael (*A* 1907–1964)
Churchill, Winston (*E* 1874–1965)
Dana, Richard Henry (*E* 1815–82)
Halliburton, Richard (*A* 1900–39)
Machiavelli, Niccolo (*It* 1469–1527)
Paine, Thomas (*E* 1737–1809)

Rousseau, Jean-Jacques (*F* 1712–78)
Swift, Jonathan (*E* 1667–1745)
Thoreau, Henry D. (*A* 1817–62)
Vanzetti, Bartolomeo (*It* 1888–1927)
Voltaire (*F* 1694–1778)
Wordsworth, Dorothy (*E* 1771–1855)

Short Stories

Algren, Nelson (*A* 1909–)
Anderson, Sherwood (*A* 1876–1941)
Benét, Stephen V. (*A* 1898–1943)
Bierce, Ambrose (*A* 1842–1914?)
Bradford, Roark (*A* 1896–1948)
Henry, O. (*A* 1867–1910)
Jackson, Shirley (*A* 1919–65)
Kafka, Franz (*G* 1883–1924)
Lardner, Ring (*A* 1885–1933)
Lawrence, D. H. (*E* 1885–1930)
Leacock, Stephen (*C* 1869–1944)

Mann, Thomas (*G* 1875–1955)
Maupaussant, Guy de (*F* 1850–93)
Milne, A. A. (*E* 1882–1956)
Morley, Christopher (*E* 1890–1957)
O'Hara, John (*A* 1905–)
Poe, Edgar Allen (*A* 1809–49)
Porter, Katherine Anne (*A* 1894–)
Thurber, James (*A* 1894–1961)
Updike, John (*A* 1932–)

Novels

Bellow, Saul (*A* 1915–)
Buck, Pearl (*A* 1892–)

Capote, Truman (*A* 1924–)
Carroll, Lewis (*E* 1832–1898)

Conrad, Joseph (*Po-E* 1857–1924)

Crane, Stephen (*A* 1871–1900)

Defoe, Daniel (*E* 1660–1731)

Dickens, Charles (*E* 1812–70)

Dostoevsky, Feodor (*R* 1821–81)

Dos Passos, John (*A* 1896–)

Doyle, Arthur C. (*E* 1859–1930)

Fast, Howard (*A* 1914–)

Faulkner, William (*A* 1897–1962)

Fielding, Henry (*E* 1707–54)

Fitzgerald, F. Scott (A 1896–1940)

Galsworthy, John (*E* 1867–1933)

Hardy, Thomas (*E* 1840–1928)

Hawthorne, Nathaniel (*A* 1804–64)

Hemingway, Ernest (*A* 1898–1961)

James, Henry (*A* 1843–1916)

Lewis, Sinclair (*A* 1885–1951)

London, Jack (*A* 1876–1916)

Maugham, W. Somerset (*E* 1874–1965)

Melville, Herman (*A* 1819–91)

Michener, James (*A* 1907–)

Orwell, George (*E* 1903–50)

Peacock, Thomas L. (*E* 1785–1866)

Salinger, J. D. (*A* 1919–)

Shulman, Max (*A* 1919–)

Steinbeck, John (*A* 1902–)

Stevenson, Robert L. (*A* 1850–94)

Tolstoy, Leo (*R* 1828–1910)

Twain, Mark (*A* 1835–1910)

Warren, Robert P. (*A* 1905–)

Wells, H. G. (*E* 1866–1916)

Wolfe, Thomas (*A* 1900–38)

POETRY

Blake, William (*E* 1757–1827)

Browning, Elizabeth B. (*E* 1806–61)

Browning, Robert (*E* 1812–89)

Burns, Robert (*Sc* 1759–96)

Byron, Lord, G. G. (*E* 1788–1824)

Chaucer, Geoffrey (*E* 1343–1400)

Ciardi, John (*A* 1916–)

Coleridge, Samuel (*E* 1772–1834)

De La Mare, Walter (*E* 1873–1956)

Dickinson, Emily (*A* 1830–86)

Donne, John (*E* 1573–1631)

Dryden, John (*E* 1631–1700)

Eliot, T. S. (*A-E* 1888–1965)

Frost, Robert (*A* 1875–1963)

Gilbert, W. S. (*E* 1836–1911)

Goethe, von, J. W. (*G* 1749–1832)

Gray, Thomas (*E* 1716–71)

Holmes, Oliver W. (*A* 1809–94)

Housman, A. E. (*E* 1859–1936)

Hughes, Langston (*A* 1902–)

Jeffers, Robinson (*A* 1887–1961)

Keats, John (*E* 1795–1821)

Lanier, Sidney (*A* 1842–81)

Lindsay, Vachael (*A* 1879–1931)

MacLeish, Archibald (*A* 1892–)

Marvell, Andrew (*E* 1621–78)

Masters, Edgar Lee (*A* 1869–1950)

Millay, Edna St. V. (*A* 1892–1950)

Milton, John (*E* 1608–74)

Nash, Ogden (*A* 1902–   )
Omar Khayyam (*P* died c. 1123)
Parker, Dorothy (*A* 1893–   )
Robinson, E. A. (*A* 1869–1935)
Sandburg, Carl (*A* 1878–   )
Shapiro, Karl (*A* 1913–   )
Shelley, Percy B. (*E* 1792–1822)
Stevens, Wallace (*A* 1879–1955)

Tennyson, Alfred, Lord
   (*E* 1809–92)
Thomas, Dylan (*W* 1914–53)
Whitman, Walt (*A* 1819–92)
Wordsworth, William (*E* 1770–
   1850)
Yeats, Williams B. (*I-E* 1865–
   1939)

DRAMA

Albee, Edward (*A* 1928–   )
Anderson, Maxwell (*A* 1888–
   1959)
Anouilh, Jean (*F* 1910–   )
Buchner, Georg (*G* 1813–37)
Chekhov, Anton (*R* 1860–1904)
Connelly, Marc (*A* 1890–   )
Euripides (*Gr* 480–407 B.C.)
Garcia Lorca, F. (*S* 1899–1935)
Giraudoux, Jean (*F* 1882–1944)
Gogol, Nikolai (*R* 1809–52)
Goldoni, Carlo (*It* 1707–93)
Green, Paul (*A* 1894–   )
Ibsen, Henrik (*N* 1828–1906)
Johnson, Ben (*E* 1572–1637)
Maeterlinck, Maurice (*B* 1862–
   1949)
Marlowe, Christopher (*E* 1564–
   93)
Miller, Arthur (*A* 1915–   )
Molière (*F* 1622–73)

Molnar, Ferenc (*H* 1878–1952)
O'Casey, Sean (*I* 1880–1963)
Odets, Clifford (*A* 1906–63)
O'Neill, Eugene (*A* 1888–1953)
Pirandello, Luigi (*It* 1867–1936)
Robinson, Lennox (*I* 1886–1958)
Rostand, Edmond (*F* 1868–
   1918)
Saroyan, William (*A* 1908–   )
Shakespeare, William (*E* 1564–
   1616)
Shaw, George Bernard (*I-E*
   1856–1950)
Sheridan, Richard B. (*E* 1759–
   1816)
Sophocles (*Gr* 496–406 B.C.)
Strindberg, August (*Sw* 1849–
   1912)
Wilde, Oscar (*I-E* 1854–1900)
Wilder, Thornton (*A* 1897–   )
Williams, Tennessee (*A* 1914–   )

SUGGESTED ASSIGNMENTS

The three reading assignments that follow have been prepared
with an understanding that you are learning to read aloud in a
course of speech fundamentals. If the full term is given to reading
aloud, your instructor may well choose to see that your development as a reader does not go neglected for want of additional assignments.

1. Prepare a three-minute reading of a narrative prose selection, preferably a travel adventure or similar type of writing that has a strong story-line. The reading will be preceeded by a two-minute introduction to the selection chosen for the reading. The introduction should reflect those items (listed in Chapter Nine) that are pertinent to the selection. The reading, of course, will be dedicated to increasing the audience's interest as the story unfolds.

2. You will have a partner for this assignment. A brief introduction to a prose or drama selection involving one or more characters will be followed by a four-minute reading. When the reading is completed, your partner will inform the class of the interpretation which he had developed prior to your reading. The class will then comment on the two interpretations (yours and your partner's) with special reference to your reading.

3. The time required for the reading of a lyric poem may be brief. The introduction might well be used to explain the backgrounds of the poem or poet. The reading will reflect those qualities for which the lyric is noted: music of the language, rhythm, and simplicity, among other considerations.